THIS BOOK IS ALL ABOUT **RIDICULOUS** THINKING FOR SUPERFAST LEARNING

SELF HELP

COMPLETE
PERSONALITY
DEVELOPMENT
COURSE

MEMORY
MIND
& BODY

DYNAMIC
Memory Methods

Tips for Becoming a Billionaire
THINK BIG
BECOME
BIG
Realize Your Dreams with Elan!
Tarun Engineer

MIND
POSITIVE
LIFE
POSITIVE
PRACTICAL TIPS FOR
GETTING SUCCESSFUL
AND POSITIVE LIFE

NOTHING
IS
IMPOSSIBLE

HOW TO
EXCEL
WHEN
CHIPS ARE
DOWN

HOW TO
SUCCEED
IN LIFE

SUCCESS
MANTRA

UNLOCK
THE DOOR TO SUCCESS

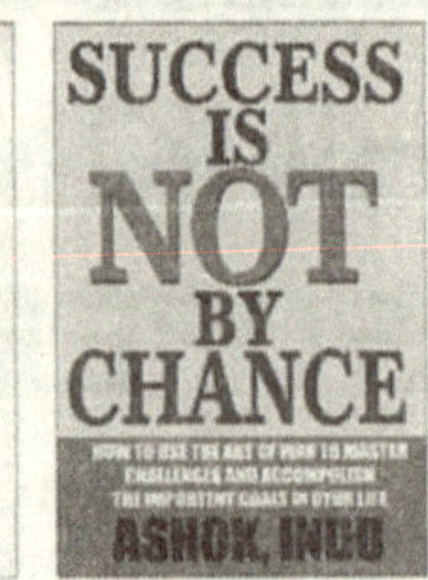
SUCCESS
IS
NOT
BY
CHANCE
ASHOK, INDU

Perfect Mantras
for Succeeding in
Network Marketing
Surya Sinha

TO WRITE
YOUR OWN
DESTINY

Dr. UJJWAL PATNI
GREAT WORDS
WIN HEARTS

The Bitter Truths of
NETWORK
MARKETING
Dr. Ujjwal Patni

Power of
Positive
Thinking

Vocabulary @ 100 Words/Hr

Scientific Memory Techniques For Super Fast Learning

Biswaroop Roy Chowdhury
National Memory Record Holder
(Limca Book Of Records)

Mahavir Jain
Youngest NLP & Memory Trainer

Publisher : **Diamond Pocket Books (P) Ltd.**

X-30, Okhla Industrial Area, Phase-II
New Delhi-110020
Phone : 011-40712200
E-mail : sales@dpb.in
Website : www.diamondbook.in

Vocabulary @ 100 Words/Hr

By : Biswaroop Roy Chowdhury

To

My Parents

who have been

my source of inspiration

for creative writing

Acknowledgments

I thank to the persons who inspired me to work on vocabulary and also promoted this unique way of learning around their surroundings.

Some of them are-

Mr. Avinash Agarwal of **aiets.com,**

Mr K. Siddharth of CENDAR,

Mr. Neeraj Agarwal of Sachdeva Coaching,

Mr. K.M. Gupta of Academy of Commerce

Deepak Ghosh of Brand Stewards.

ABOUT THE AUTHORS

Biswaroop Roy Chowdhury

Biswaroop Roy Chowdhury, an engineer by education, the National Memory Record Holder (*Limca Book of Records*), is a leading name in the field of Memory Training. His techniques are appreciated by students, teachers, corporate houses, housewives, professionals, etc. and widely covered by the National Print and Electronic Media like *The Times of India, The Hindustan Times, The Tribune, The Indian Express, The Hindu, Jansatta, Punjab Kesari, Navbharat Times, Sandhya Times, Dainik Jagran, Life Positive, Junior Science Refresher, The Competition Master, Grihalaxmi, Civil Services Chronicle, Zee News, Aankho Dekhi, (DD-1), All India Radio, The Statesman, The Telegraph, The Asian Age, Dainik Bhasker, Jain T.V., Navbharat, Sandhya Times, indiatimes.com, The Pioneer, Rashtriya Sahara*, etc. He can be contacted at

Delhi, Mobile : (O) 9811139474/www.dynamicmemory.com

Mahavir Jain

Mahavir Jain, aged 27, is a behavioural specialist and youngest NLP & Memory trainer of India with years of professional experience. This mechanical engineering graduate from Regional Enginering Kurukshetra with working experience of reputed automobile companies of Eicher Ltd. & LML Ltd. quitted his engineering profession and deliberately picked up a wonderful and exciting field of brain & human engineering. In his young age, he has benefitted thousands of individuals, families.

Mr Jain is serving as a Mind Management Consultant for the various colleges, corporates. He is the memory consultant for The Hindustan Times.

An acclaimed speaker, trainer, he is recognised for his innovative and enlightening presentations. Today he conducts his workshops, seminars under the banner of MASTERMIND-POSITIVE ZONE®.

Smart and suave, Mr. Jain is endowed with a penetrative and creative mind, amazing spontaneity. Apart from Memory, NLP training and Motivational pragrammes, he also enjoys his life in reading, writing. He is writing some other books on 'CREATIVITY-a suucess formula', & 'NLP for Students.'

He can be contacted at

Delhi at Mobile-9811317599, 91-5225156,
5422101, 95-1275-38286.

Media comments

"He has got the Mantra to develop brain."

October 2, 1997, Dainik Tribune

"Biswaroop is a memory genius with a penchant for breaking records."

May 18, 1997, Indain Express

"Today in the arena of cut-throat competition memory development techniques customized by Biswaroop, a pioneer in the field of memory development can surely resue the overburdened students."

All India Radio, Yuv Vani (August 4, 1999)

"Once you are through with Dynamic Memory Methods, you might well be on the road to a better memory."

Life Positive, August 1999

"Biswaroop, the memory master demostrated his findings on memory principles by helping audience learn a complex sequences easily."

The Asian Age, January 9, 2001

"Biswaroop knows how to make the grey cells work."

The Times of India, January 7, 2001

"Combining the ancient wisdom and latest findings, Biswaroop has developed five techniques — memory language (shape learning), phonetic method (sound learning), personal meaning system (linking method), radiant thinking and advanced mnemonics system."

The Telegraph, January 10, 2001

"Biswaroop Roy Chowdhury, the man behind the books like *Dyanimic Memory Methods,* is indeed a genius."

The Hindustan Times, February 18, 2001

"Biswaroop has memorized 600 years of the calendar."

India Today, January 22, 2001

CONTENTS

LIST OF 400 WORDS

1. Abase
2. Abstruse
3. Acclimatize
4. Acturial
5. Adroit
6. Aegis
7. Affected
8. Affluence
9. Affront
10. Alacrity
11. Allay
12. Altercation
13. Altruistic
14. Ambivalence
15. Ameliorate
16. Apposite
17. Ardous
18. Arrack
19. Asinine
20. Assiduous
21. Astute
22. Attrition
23. Augment
24. Apprise
25. Assay
26. Appease
27. Avarice
28. Abrogate
29. Abstinence
30. Acclaim
31. Accord
32. Acme
33. Acrimonious
34. Anchorite
35. Alchemy
36. Amnesia
37. Abate
38. Accede
39. Anathema
40. Appal
41. Baleful
42. Bedizen
43. Belabour
44. Belittle
45. Bellicose
46. Blandishment
47. Banal
48. Bedlam
49. Behmoth
50. Brazen
51. Bulwark
52. Bamboozle
53. Bandy
54. Baroque
55. Beatitude
56. Bizzare
57. Beguile
58. Benison
59. Bismirch
60. Bibulous
61. Blight
62. Bluster
63. Bohemian
64. Bovine
65. Browbeat
66. Bumptious
67. Bolster
68. Burgeon
69. Bleagured
70. Bout
71. Cabal
72. Cadence
73. Cajole
74. Callow
75. Canny
76. Canvass
77. Capacious
78. Capricious
79. Cardinal
80. Careen
81. Carnage
82. Cataclysm
83. Celerity
84. Censure
85. Certitude
86. Chagrin
87. Chequred
88. Chimerical
89. Cipher
90. Circuitous
91. Circumspect
92. Clairvoyance
93. Cliche
94. Cogent
95. Coerce
96. Compendium
97. Conflagration
98. Copious
99. Covert
100. Credulous
101. Culinary
102. Cull
103. Culpable
104. Cynosure
105. Calumny
106. Candid

107. Captious
108. Carp
109. Cartographer
110. Cathartic
111. Caveat
112. Charlatan
113. Cherubic
114. Cogitate
115. Commiserate
116. Conjecture
117. Contagious
118. Corroborate
119. Cupidity
120. Curry
121. Chary
122. Colander
123. Cower
124. Cursory
125. Condescend
126. Cache
127. Canon
128. Cantankerous
129. Chaff
130. Choleric
131. Concomitant
132. Conjugal
133. Culmination
134. Crabbed
135. Cryptic
136. Cul-de-sac
137. Carmine
138. Cognomen
139. Digress
140. Diligence
141. Dipsomaniac
142. Disavowal
143. Disconcert
144. Discord
145. Discursive
146. Disinterested
147. Diurnal
148. Dicey
149. Deadpan
150. Dirge
151. Distrain
152. Dotage
153. Dyspepsia
154. Deranged
155. Deride
156. Descant
157. Diaphanous
158. Dilletante
159. Disport
160. Dregs
161. Dubious
162. Dulcet
163. Defalcate
164. Deleterious
165. Derelict
166. Despondency
167. Detente
168. Detrimental
169. Diabolical
170. Diffidence
171. Dissemble
172. Dormant
173. Draconian
174. Dolorous
175. Decadence
176. Decimate
177. Devolve
178. Diatribe
179. Didactic
180. Exculpate
181. Eccentric
182. Eclectic
183. Elixir
184. Encumber
185. Enigma
186. Eschew
187. Eulogy
188. Exigency
189. Extol
190. Efulgent
191. Emollient
192. Enormity
193. Espouse
194. Extricate
195. Ebullient
196. Enervate
197. Enjoin
198. Enunciate
199. Ephemeral
200. Epitaph
201. Equitable
202. Excision
203. Extirpate
204. Extraneous
205. Engender
206. Earthy
207. Embellish
208. Ennui
209. Flippant
210. Fulminate
211. Febrile
212. Fealty
213. Felicity
214. Fatuous
215. Firebrand
216. Facile
217. Fortitude

218. Fulsome
219. Fallacy
220. Fatalism
221. Fecund
222. Figurine
223. Faux pass
224. Functionary
225. Fiasco
226. Gerrymander
227. Garrulous
228. Germane
229. Glean
230. Glut
231. Gourmand
232. Grueling
233. Gambit
234. Genuflect
235. Gadfly
236. Gossamer
237. Graduated
238. Gullible
239. Gyrate
240. Gregarious
241. Harangue
242. Halcyon
243. Hiatus
244. Hirsute
245. Histrionic
246. Homily
247. Horrendous
248. Hortatory
249. Highfautin
250. Horology
251. Idyllic
252. Imminent
253. Impeccable
254. Impinge
255. Inclement
256. Idiosyncracy
257. Imbroglio
258. Impolitic
259. Impugn
260. Incipient
261. Incursion
262. Indefatigable
263. Indemnity
264. Inebrity
265. Innocuous
266. Insouciant
267. Invective
268. Incontinent
269. Insipid
270. Insurmountable
271. Irate
272. Juxtapose
273. Jaunty
274. Jocund
275. Jettison
276. Jeremiad
277. Jeer
278. Jersey
279. Jib
280. Jape
281. Japanoica
282. Jalopy
283. Jangle
284. Jagged
285. Jodhpurs
286. Juror
287. Kleptomania
288. Killjoy
289. Knacker
290. Lassitude
291. List
292. Lampoon
293. Latitude
294. Misnomer
295. Limbo
296. Loopy
297. Labyrinth
298. Laconic
299. Lapidary
300. Ludicurous
301. Macabre
302. Moribund
303. Motility
304. Machination
305. Malinger
306. Manger
307. Mercenary
308. Mercurial
309. Mete
310. Meticulous
311. Militate
312. Misgiving
313. Misnomer
314. Mountebank
315. Mundane
316. Munificient
317. Myopia
318. Mortified
319. Machievellian
320. Martinet
321. Maudlin
322. Minutiae
323. Moratorium
324. Nebulous
325. Nettle
326. Nexus
327. Necromancy
328. Noisome

329. Nostrum
330. Nefarious
331. Nonchalance
332. Nepotism
333. Overt
334. Opulence
335. Ostensible
336. Ostracize
337. Odyssey
338. Opportune
339. Ostentatious
340. Oniomania
341. Obfuscate
342. Occident
343. Ordain
344. Pandemonium
345. Parsimonium
346. Perfidious
347. Petrify
348. Polemic
349. Preposterous
350. Puerile
351. Ratify
352. Ravenous
353. Recalcitrant
354. Redolent
355. Refrain
356. Repertoire
357. Rider
358. Rife
359. Ruminate
360. Rankle
361. Rectitude
362. Reticent
363. Reverie
364. Risque
365. Rabid
366. Rapacious
367. Ratiocination
368. Recondite
369. Redress
370. Remonstrate
371. Reprehensible
372. Restive
373. Rhapsodize
374. Rancor
375. Recant
376. Refractory
377. Relegate
378. Repartee
379. Replenish
380. Resurgent
381. Retrench
382. Ribald
383. Rotundity
384. Rubicund
385. Randy
386. Ricochet
387. Rookie
388. Salacious
389. Sinuous
390. Sojourn
391. Sedulous
392. Slander
393. Spectral
394. Subjugate
395. Supplant
396. Tenacious
397. Torpor
398. Tyro
399. Tremulous
400. Thwart

In each human brain there are estimated one million-million (1000000 000 000) brain cells

Let's Test Your Vocabulary

Before you start this exciting journey of learning 400 words in 4 hours through scientific learning techniques of subconscious mind, we would like to take a test of words. This will help you to find out what your present vocabulary level is. This will be an interesting experiment for you to analyse your vocabulary.

When you would be doing the test you would realise that with some of the words you had familiarity but you are not able to recollect right now. After the book is over you will able to detect the weak points in learning method of your vocabulary. And this is the right book which has designed to remove those wrong method of remembering.

We have given a new idea, a new method which we call very creative for building vocabulary and the techniques of this book are based on this new approach of visualisation.

Now you prepare yourself for the test. The rules for taking these tests are simple. You will see there all 10 words in each test. After each word there are four words or phrases lettered a, b, c, d. Check that word or phrase that you think is closest in meaning to the given word. Let's take a sample.

Dormant— (a) Inactive (b) Active (c) Courage (d) Cruel

In this case you will mark 'Inactive' as being nearest in meaning to "Dormant". Readers are requested not to do too much guessing. You are also advised not to use hit & trial method. If you do by 'guessing or hit & trial method', you will unable to find out a good judgement of your present vocabulary.

After you have finished these 5 tests turn to page 22 & check your result against the correct answers that are given there.

TEST—1

1. Acclimatize
   (a) to adjust with the climate
   (b) to change the climate
   (c) to migrate from cold to winter place
   (d) to save the crops from rain

2. Affluence
   (a) poverty (b) wealth
   (c) a creation (d) a cancellation
3. Nexus
   (a) A fracture (b) An agreement
   (c) A connection (d) A punishment
4. Petrify
   (a) to make somebody frightened
   (b) to deceive
   (c) to provoke
   (d) to catch easily
5. Impeccable
   (a) incidental (b) faultless
   (c) mistakes (d) careless
6. Gourmand
   (a) A person eats too much (b) A coward
   (c) A courageous man (d) Wise person
7. Dogmatic
   (a) Claiming without right (b) Uninteresting
   (c) Insisting one's belief (d) Proud & disdainful
8. Belittle
   (a) to consider equally (b) to fortune
   (c) to degrade (d) to sacrifice
9. Augment
   (a) to add (b) to excite
   (c) to cut (d) to fly
10. Digress
   (a) to visit a place (b) to convince
   (c) to improve (d) to go away from main topic.

This was an easy test & I hope you have the positive feeling that you did this fairly good. Most of the literate people are able to do well this test.

TEST—2

1. Altercation
   (a) an agreement (b) a noisy quarrel
   (c) punishment (d) romantic story

2. Acme
   (a) highest point
   (b) bottom
   (c) rough stone
   (d) swollen & thick area of a body
3. Flippant
   (a) feeling of well being
   (b) victory
   (c) changeable
   (d) confusion
4. Contagious
   (a) spreads through touching
   (b) contractaction of bones
   (c) expansion of air
   (d) conspiracy
5. Candid
   (a) hiding
   (b) honest & frank
   (c) sticky
   (d) swollen
6. Hiatus
   (a) sinful
   (b) a order
   (c) a warning
   (d) a gap or difference
7. Glut
   (a) moderate
   (b) scarcity
   (c) over abundance
   (d) demand
8. Insipid
   (a) sumptuous
   (b) tasteless
   (c) creative
   (d) boastful
9. Laconic
   (a) detail
   (b) brief
   (c) corrupted
   (d) interrupted
10. Ratify
   (a) to verify
   (b) to catch
   (c) to flatter
   (d) to hesitate

This is not very complicated test but little harder than previous one. You would have missed 2-3 words out of these words.

TEST - 3

1. Alacrity
   (a) lazy manner
   (b) carelessness
   (c) promptness
   (d) enjoyment
2. Ardous
   (a) hard
   (b) brief
   (c) eary
   (d) slow

3. Bandy
   (a) to honour (b) to discuss lightly
   (c) to battle (d) to deviate
4. Banal
   (a) common (b) winding
   (c) desire (d) Injury
5. Cupidity
   (a) desire for love (b) desire for wealth
   (c) feeling of boldness (d) desire for revenge
6. Diligence
   (a) perfection (b) hardwork
   (c) familiarity (d) literacy
7. Calumny
   (a) a false statement (b) a news column
   (c) government (d) cry extremely
8. Credulous
   (a) doubtful (b) humorous
   (c) arrogant (d) believable
9. Nebulous
   (a) not clear (b) very sure
   (c) consistent (d) confident
10. Leeway
   (a) stick to something (b) freedom to move
   (c) exhaustation (d) control

Some words in this test are more difficult but people who have fairly rich vocabulary comfortably qualify this test. If you are able to recollect the meanings of 9 words out of 10, you assume you have superior vocabulary.

TEST - 4

1. Beguile
   (a) to cheat (b) to trick to attract
   (c) to encourage (d) to make angry
2. Lapidary
   (a) a teacher (b) a rider
   (c) a worker (d) a businessman
3. Occident
   (a) epidemic (b) romantic story
   (c) western past of world (d) earthquake

4. Preposterous
   (a) Absurd & dirty (b) clean & clear
   (b) reddlish & bluish (d) sticky & harmful
5. Ruminate
   (a) to sleep deeply (b) to think over
   (c) to criticize (d) to placate
6. Rhapsody
   (a) great enthusiasm in writing & speech
   (b) jealousy with neighbour
   (c) great demand of money
   (d) feeling of anger.
7. Malinger
   (a) to overcome (b) to accommodate
   (c) to pretend to be ill (d) to shiver out of fear
8. Insouciant
   (a) carefree, free from worries (b) Tensed & worried
   (c) indifferent (d) political agenda
9. Fiasco
   (a) success (b) failure
   (c) agreement (d) visit to an historical place.
10. Harangue
   (a) to criticize loudly (b) to hide the facts
   (c) to conspire (d) to feel exhausted

This test is very difficult. Very few persons can score 10 out of 10. Don't be disheartened if are not scoring good in this. We shall tell you the technique of remembering the meaning of these words. They you'll be able to recall the meaning easily.

TEST- 5

This is test which contains highly typical words. If you are able to recall the meaning of these words. You will be a person of super vocabulary. It will prove you that you have extraordinary vocabulary. Don't worry if these words are unfamiliar to you or even miss you to recall. This is because you remembered easier through worry method of memorising. By the time you will finish this book & learn the technique you will comfortably tell the meanings.

1. Exiguous
   (a) hard to understand
   (b) a definite order
   (c) scanty or small around
   (d) serious illness
2. Machination
   (a) A sudden demand
   (b) A resolution
   (c) a complicated plan
   (d) serious illness
3. Moratorium
   (a) Stadium
   (b) conference
   (c) unconsciousness
   (d) a legal suspension or delay
4. Descant
   (a) to walk fast
   (b) to discuss fully
   (b) to bask
   (d) to right
5. Rookie
   (a) a golf stick
   (b) Uncertainty
   (c) Inexperienced person
   (d) Confusion
6. Condescend
   (a) to rise above
   (b) to come down
   (c) to fell down
   (d) to speak loudly
7. Dyspepsia
   (a) a temporary relief
   (b) Order
   (c) pain caused by indigestion of food
   (d) shock
8. Cul-de-sac
   (a) to welcome insincerely
   (b) to trap
   (c) to criticize
   (d) to lessen the pain.
9. Diurnal
   (a) active during the day
   (b) entering without ticket
   (c) top point
   (d) insulting
10. Detente
   (a) business negotiation
   (b) explosion at the remote area
   (c) digress
   (d) lessening of tension between two countries

ANSWERS

TEST - 1: 1. (a), 2. (b), 3. (c), 4. (a), 5. (b), 6. (a), 7. (c), 8. (c), 9. (a), 10. (d)

TEST - 2: 1. (b), 2. (a), 3. (c), 4. (a), 5. (b), 6. (d), 7. (c), 8. (b), 9. (b), 10. (a)

TEST - 3: 1. (c), 2. (a), 3. (b), 4. (a), 5. (b), 6. (b), 7. (a), 8. (d), 9. (a), 10. (b)

TEST - 4: 1. (a), 2. (c), 3. (c), 4. (a), 5. (b), 6. (a), 7. (c), 8. (a), 9. (b), 10. (a)

TEST - 5: 1. (c), 2. (c), 3. (d), 4. (b), 5. (c), 6. (b), 7. (c), 8. (b), 9. (a), 10. (d)

Your Vocabulary Rating

TEST - 1: 10-9 correct - excellent
8-7 correct - good to fair
6 & under - poor

TEST - 2: 10-8 correct - excellent
7-6 correct - good to fair
5 & under - poor

TEST - 3: 10-7 correct - excellent
6-4 correct - good
4 & under - poor

TEST- 4: 10-6 correct - excellent
5-4 correct - good
3 & under - poor

TEST - 5: 10-5 correct - excellent
4-3 correct - good
2 & under fair to poor

Now count the total number of correct answers that you scored in the above 5 tests of 50 words & then look below for your vocabulary rating.

50-46 - extraordinary
45-40 - excellent
40-30 - very good
29 - 26 - average
25 & under poor

This ratings of these tests will give you a helpful picture of your present vocabulary rating. The techniques which have mentioned in this book to memorise typical vocabulary through visualisation will bring an extraordinary change in the method learning the words.

HOW TO USE THIS BOOK?

Hello friends,

Lets be precise and to the point from the very beginning because the race is against time. The necessary things you must have before you go beyond the star (*) mark are

1. Pencil 2. Stop clock.

*I am sure you have got the above two required things with you.

This book can actually help you in learning new & unheard typical English words at the speed of 100 words /hr. subject to the condition that you follow strictly following suggestions.

(1) First four chapters are the foundation of the new scientific technique for learning, so don't be in hurry in reading them.

Ensure that you are 100% clear about the content and the message of 1st chapter before moving further.

(2) Now to go through the memory chart- 'Remember' several time before you start memorising the words using memory techniques.

(3) This book should be treated as a work book. Don't hesitate to appear in the given tests.

(4) Time your stop watch and write down (in the space provided) the time you take in learning a set of 25 words.

(5) After every set (of 25 words) give yourself a rest of 10 minutes.

(6) Follow the following schedule.

DAY 1: Read, understand and absorb the first 4 chapters and also understand the REMEMBER chart at the end of the book.

DAY 2: Revise again what you read the first day and appear for the first vocab. test.

DAY 3: Set the stop watch and attempt to learn the first set of 25 words. Note the total time taken in learning (not reading) the first set (in the space provided). Now appear for the given test.

Take a break of 10 minutes.

Reset your stop watch and attempt for the second set. Note down the time taken and appear for 2nd set test.

DAY 4: Step 1: Revise those 50 words you learnt on day 3. (Please don't skip this step.)

Step 2: Attempt for next 3 sets in the similar manner. By this time you should realise a definite improvement in your speed of learning words-meanings.

DAY 5: Step 1: Revise all the three sets which you learnt yesterday.

Step 2: Attempt next 3 sets.

DAY 6: Revise all the 200 words you learnt in last 3 days. To That's all for today!

DAY 7: Attempt next 4 sets.

DAY 8: Step 1: Revise the last 4 sets.

Step 2: Attempt next and the last 4 sets. Each set should not take more than 15 minutes.

DAY 9: Just relax and give yourself a break.

DAY 10: Go for a final revision of all the to 400 words. It should not take more than one hour.

CHAPTER- 1

MEMORY MECHANISM

What is memory? What results in the feeling of being learnt? How do we remember the things we remember? Did you ever question your memory about memory?

ANSWER

Memory is nothing but connection of new thoughts/ information with the thoughts/information which are already stored in the brain.

LAW OF ASSOCIATION

We learn a new data when it gets linked/ associated with the data which is already stored in the brain. And that linkage or connection is called *memory*. For instance, you happen to visit your childhood school building. The key to the recall is the connection of your experience with the school building.

THE CHAIN METHOD

Let us say you want to learn the following list of words in the same order.

1. Dog	2. Shoes	3. Movie
4. Dragon	5. Cycle	6. Telephone
7. Pen	8. Cold drink	9. Tiger
10. Tape recorder		

METHOD-I

One way of learning this is by repeating it till it is learnt. It may take about 25 repetitions which may ensure a perfect recall even after 2-3 days.

METHOD-II

The second way is to form an association between the words. For example :

Imaging a DOG wearing SHOES and going for a MOVIE of a DRAGON is riding a CYCLE. The cycle hits a TELEPHONE BOOTH. A person repairs the telephone with the tip of a PEN. Now think that the pen is filled with COLD DRINK and not ink. You are serving cold drink to a TIGER. The tiger is dancing to the tune of a TAPE RECORDER.

Do you need to read it again?

Isn't that simple? Surely Method-II is more efficient than Method I but one thing is common in both the methods, that is association. In the first method the words got associated automatically/ subconsciously with the other stored information of the brain. Hence, you may confuse the order later on. While in Method-II you made a deliberate attempt to learn the words with conscious association.

Conscious association is better than subconscious or no association.

CONCLUSION

Always try to connect the new information you want to learn with something (else).

CHAPTER - 2

IMAGINATION — A PERFECT RETENTION METHOD

Every invention is first invented in imagination then in reality. The imagination is literally the workshop wherein are fashioned all plans created by man. Man's only limitation, within reason, lies in his development and use of his imagination. Imagination is an intangible force, but it has more power than the physical brain that gives birth to it. It has the power to live on even after the brain that creates it has returned to dust.

Use this power in learning.

VISUALIZATION

Whatever you read, try to convert that into a picture and visualize it. Our eye memory is stronger by 20 times than the ear memory since the nerves connecting brains to eye are stronger by 20 times than nerves connecting ears to brain. This method can be best used in subjects like History. For instance, if you need to learn all about the Harappan civilization, read, understand and construct the civilization mentally in your mind. Try to live in that.

Always ensure that whatever you read, you have something in picture to relate to. Hearing makes us learn the thing. Seeing and imagining the same makes us remember the information for long.

Visualization has helped me in making a national record in memory for perfect retention.

CHAPTER - 3

MEMORY LINK—FOR LEARNING FOREIGN LANGUAGES

The salesman who speaks the language of his prospective customer has such an enormous advantage over his competitor who does not that, there can hardly be any doubt about the comparative success of their respective business trips.

What is the easiet way to learn a foreign language?

ANSWER :

The Memory link method.

For example, if you want to learn that the French word *jeu* means *game*. You can do it simply by thinking of *joy* as a link which is similiar in sound of the French word *jeu* and associated by thinking getting joy out of playing a game. This kind of thinking is sufficient to recall the foreign word whenever we need it. Moreover, experience shows that after a while the linking word will vanish from our mind and the association between the French and the English word will become so strong that we shall recall the other directly and without the help of the linking words.

EXAMPLE 1:

The French word *lagare* means *railway station.* We can learn it by simply thinking of *line guard* which is similar in sound of *lagare*. Now link it to the meaning by thinking a *line guard of railway station.*

EXAMPLE 2:

The Spanish word *el libro* means *book.*

Step 1: A similar sounding word for *el libro* could be *library.*

Step 2: Connecting the word library with the actual meaning *book* by thinking library is a collection of *books* in organized manner for sharing.

EXAMPLE 3:

Latin word *poena* means *punishment.*

Step 1: Similar sounding word—*Peon*

Step 2: Connection—Peon got *punishment* for his mischief.

Remember, it is not just sufficient to understand the memory sentence for retantian of the words and their meanings rather you must imagine the complete thing. For instance in example 3 you should be able to see a *Peon* wearing brown uniform, is hiding a very important red coloured document and is thrown out of the office. That's his punishment for his mischief.

CHAPTER - 4

MEMORY LINK METHOD—FOR VOCABULARY

Vocabulary plays a very important role specially in competitive examinations like MBA, GMAT, etc.

The rules which we have applied to the vocabularies of foreign language can likewise be applied to words in English that are unfamiliar to us. Theoretically speaking, it does not make much difference whether we hear a Spanish word or an English word for the first time. If we do not know a particular word, we must do something about it and the best way to remember it is to find a linking word.

For example lets say the WORD is *Abase* and the meaning of the the word is *to degrade*. Now it would be easier for us to store it in our memory bank if we think of some similiar sounding word. For instance BASEMENT sounds similiar to the word *Abase*.

Now this BASEMENT would work as a KEY to remember if we think of a sentence connecting BASEMENT and *to degrade*. So the MEMORY LINK sentence could be *we took him in the basement & degraded him.*

Next time whenever you come across the word Abase automatically it will remind you of the similiar sounding word "basement" which will give you the clue about hte meaning of "ABASE" through the MEMORY LINK sentence "We took him in the basement & degraded him."

1.	Word	:	**Abase** (*v*)
	Meaning	:	*to lower in position; to degrade*
	Key	:	BASEMENT
	Memory link	:	We took him in the BASEMENT & *degraded* him.
	Usage	:	Some cowardice abased the soldiers image.
2.	Word	:	**Abstruse** (*adj*)
	Meaning	:	*difficult to understand*
	Key	:	TRUE
	Memory link	:	TRUTH is always *difficult to understand.*
	Usage	:	Abstruse argument / topic.
3.	Word	:	**Acclimatize** (*v*)
	Meaning	:	*adjust with climate or with any condition*
	Key	:	CLIMATE
	Memory link	:	I cannot *adjust* in this CLIMATE.
	Usage	:	Australian cricket team arrive two days early in order to acclimatize.
4.	Word	:	**Acturial** (*adj*)
	Meaning	:	*calculating*
	Key	:	ACTUAL
	Memory link	:	To *calculate* ACTUAL result, you need a calculator.
	Usage	:	His acturial skill is very good.

5.	Word	:	**Adroit** (*adj*)
	Meaning	:	*skillful*
	Key	:	AD-ADVERTISEMENT – WROTE
	Memory link	:	The person who WROTE Cadbury's ADVERTISEMENT script was very *skillful*.
	Usage	:	He succeeded by his adroit diplomacy.
6.	Word	:	**Aegis** (*n*)
	Meaning	:	*protection; support*
	Key	:	AGE
	Memory link	:	Children's *support* is required in the old AGE.
	Usage	:	Facilities were provided under the aegis of Redcross Society.
7.	Word	:	**Affected** (*adj*)
	Meaning	:	*artificial; pretended*
	Key	:	AFFECT
	Memory link	:	He lost all his property but in *artificial* manner he showed that it didn't AFFECT on him.
	Usage	:	An affected smile on his face.
8.	Word	:	**Affluence** (*n*)
	Meaning	:	*wealth, abundance*
	Key	:	FLUENCY
	Memory link	:	His FLUENCY in english was very good. So he earned a lot of *wealth*.
	Usage	:	Live a life of affluence.

9.	Word	:	**Affront** (*n*)
	Meaning	:	*insult; offense*
	Key	:	FRONT
	Memory link	:	We should not *insult* anybody in FRONT of somebody else.
	Usage	:	His speech was an affront to the members.
10.	Word	:	**Alacrity** (*n*)
	Meaning	:	*cheerful; promptness; eagerness*
	Key	:	A LAC (RUPEE)
	Memory link	:	There was sudden *promptness* in his work, the moment he got ONE LAC RUPEES.
	Usage	:	He accepted her offer with alacrity.
11.	Word	:	**Allay** (*v*)
	Meaning	:	*to lessen; to calm*
	Key	:	आ ले
	Memory link	:	Don't weep & cry, आ ले and *be calm.*
	Usage	:	Allay troubles / fear.
12.	Word	:	**Altercation** (*n*)
	Meaning	:	*noisy querrel; heated dispute*
	Key	:	ALTERATION
	Memory link	:	Tailor did wrong ALTERATION of my trouser so a *noisy querrel* took place.
	Usage	:	A brief altercation with match refree.

13.	Word	:	**Altruistic** (*adj*)
	Meaning	:	*unselfishly; generous; kind*
	Key	:	ALL TRUST
	Memory link	:	The kind & generous people TRUST (ALL).
	Usage	:	Altruistic behaviour.
14.	Word	:	**Ambivalence** (*adj*)
	Meaning	:	*state of not able to decide because of emotional attitude*
	Key	:	BALANCE
	Memory link	:	I was *not able to decide* how to BALANCE my professional and personal life.
	Usage	:	Whether to go or not- an ambivalence situation.
15.	Word	:	**Ameliorate** (*v*)
	Meaning	:	*to improve; to make something better*
	Key	:	AMUL RATE
	Memory link	:	AMUL RATE as well as quality is *improving* everyday.
	Usage	:	The situation in Pakistan after war is ameliorating.
16.	Word	:	**Apposite** (*adj*)
	Meaning	:	*appropriate; fitting*
	Key	:	OPPOSITE
	Memory link	:	An *appropriate* girl lives OPPOSITE to my house.
	Usage	:	An apposite remark on him.

17.	Word	:	**Arduous** (*n*)
	Meaning	:	*tough*
	Key	:	HARD
	Memory link	:	This is a *tough* job, you will have to do lot of HARDwork.
	Usage	:	*The work is very arduous.*
18.	Word	:	**Arrack** (*v*)
	Meaning	:	*strong alcoholic drink*
	Key	:	A RACK
	Memory link	:	My brother hide *alcoholic drink* in A RACK.
	Usage	:	*Arrack is a special kind of alcoholic drink.*
19.	Word	:	**Asinine** (*adj*)
	Meaning	:	*stupid*
	Key	:	ASS NINE
	Memory link	:	Those NINE ASSES are doing *stupid* things.
	Usage	:	*Asinine behaviour.*
20.	Word	:	**Assiduous** (*adj*)
	Meaning	:	*working hard*
	Key	:	ASS DOES
	Memory link	:	ASS DOES lot of *hardwork* from day to night.
	Usage	:	An assiduous research by the scientist.

21.	Word	:	**Astute** (*adj*)
	Meaning	:	*wise; skilled*
	Key	:	A SCIENCE TUTOR
	Memory link	:	Our SCIENCE TUTOR is very *wise*.
	Usage	:	An astute lawyer / businessman.
22.	Word	:	**Attrition** (*n*)
	Meaning	:	*A gradual reduction.*
	Key	:	RATION SHOP
	Memory link	:	There was a gradual reduction of price AT RATION SHOP.
	Usage	:	A high rate of attrition in union membership.
23.	Word	:	**Augment** (*v*)
	Meaning	:	*to increase*
	Key	:	आग – MINT
	Memory link	:	*To increase* the fire, he put mint in the आग.
	Usage	:	He started to augment his income by other ways.
24.	Word	:	**Apprise** (*v*)
	Meaning	:	*to inform.*
	Key	:	PRIZE
	Memory link	:	The boy *informed* his mother when he won the PRIZE in the competition.
	Usage	:	Why didn't you apprise me about your plan ?

25.	Word	:	**Assay** (*n*)
	Meaning	:	*evaluation; analysis*
	Key	:	EASSY
	Memory link	:	The principal asked the teachers *to evaluate* the ESSAY on population carefully.
	Usage	:	Prepare an assay of a metal structure.

TIME : ___________

TEST-1 (1-25 WORDS)

I. Write down the key of the following words. For example:

Aegis	**Age**
1. Arrack	____________
2. Attrition	____________
3. Affluence	____________
4. Augment	____________
5. Apprise	____________
6. Astute	____________
7. Affected	____________
8. Acturial	____________
9. Assay	____________
10. Affront	____________

ANSWERS:

1. Rack, 2. At राशन (shop), 3. Fluency, 4. आग Mint, 5. Prize, 6. A Sc. Tutor, 7. Affect, 8. Actual, 9. Essay, 10. Front.

Now you are well enough acquainted with these words to connect each one with its proper meaning ? Would you like to do?

1. Arrack	(a) support
2. Attrition	(b) to analyse
3. Affluence	(c) pretending
4. Augment	(d) to inform
5. Apprise	(e) wise
6. Astute	(f) decrease
7. Affected	(g) alcholic drink
8. Acturial	(h) to increase
9. Assay	(i) wealth
10. Aegis	(j) calculate

ANSWERS:

1. (g), 2. (f), 3. (i), 4. (h), 5. (d), 6. (e), 7. (c), 8. (j), 9. (b), 10. (a).

III. Here is the list of 10 words with their synonyms. Tick the right one.

1. Alacrity
   (a) increase (b) spread
   (c) sureness (d) promptness

2. Allay
   (a) to become angry (b) to lessen
   (c) stupid (d) to walk

3. Abstruse
   (a) difficult to understand (b) insist
   (c) aggressive (d) improve

4. Assiduous
   (a) generous (b) dreadful
   (c) hardworking (d) shameful

5. Ameliorate
   (a) to improve (b) to affect
   (c) to degrade (d) to violate

6. Acclimatize
   (a) cause (b) adjust with climate
   (c) roomy (d) to steal

7. Adroit
   (a) wise (b) calculative
   (c) humiliate (d) aggressive

8. Altercation
   (a) support (b) difficult
   (c) noisy querrel (d) appropriate

9. Ardous
   (a) fire (b) hidden
   (c) bold (d) hard

10. Asinine

(a) wise (b) stupid

(c) aggressive (d) artificial

ANSWERS:

1. (d), 2. (b), 3. (a), 4. (c), 5. (a), 6. (b), 7. (a), 8. (c), 9. (d), 10. (b)

III. Tick the closest meaning of *italicised* word in the sentence.

1. The speaker's remark was an *affront* to the media people
   (a) insult
   (b) ençouragement
   (c) discouragement

2. ARRACK is a
   (a) poisionous metal
   (b) strong alcholic drink
   (c) a hiding place

3. The clerk job is an *ardous* job
   (a) rewarding
   (b) time consuming
   (c) hard

4. Please *apprise* him about our visit
   (a) send
   (b) inform
   (c) call

5. There was a little *altercation* with my boss
   (a) querrel
   (b) discussion
   (c) agreement

6. After the relief work, situation of Gujarat started to *ameliorate*
   (a) spoil
   (b) improve
   (c) deteriorate

7. When we *abase* somebody we try to __________ him.
   (a) support
   (b) sympathize
   (c) degard or lower him

8. He is an *astute* manager
   (a) wise
   (b) cunning
   (c) polite

9. I was in *ambivalence* situation
   (a) difficult to decide
   (b) good
   (c) resourceful

10. My boss's *acturial* skill is excellent
   (a) communication
   (b) calcualtive
   (c) interpersonal

ANSWERS:

1. (a), 2. (b), 3. (c), 4. (b), 5. (a), 6. (b), 7. (c), 8. (a), 9. (a), 10. (b)

V. Write down the meanings of the following words :

S. No.	Word	Meaning
1.	Apposite	________
2.	Affluence	________
3.	Affected	________
4.	Assay	________
5.	Aegis	________
6.	Attrition	________
7.	Affluence	________
8.	Altruistic	________
9.	Augment	________
10.	Asinine	________

ANSWERS:

1. appropriate, 2. wealth, 3. artificial, 4. to analyse, 5. support 6.decrease gradually, 7. wealth, 8. kind or generous, 9. to increase, 10. stupid.

26.	Word	:	**Appease** (*v*)
	Meaning	:	*to pacify; to relieve*
	Key	:	APPLE PIECE
	Memory link	:	Why don't you take a PIECE OF APPLE? It will *relieve your* hunger for sometime.
	Usage	:	He was trying to appease his anger/hunger.
27.	Word	:	**Avarice** (*adj*)
	Meaning	:	*greed*
	Key	:	A वारिस
	Memory link	:	All the वारिस have an intense *greed* of her property.
	Usage	:	I don't like his avarice nature.
28.	Word	:	**Abrogate** (*v*)
	Meaning	:	*to cancel; to abolish*
	Key	:	रो GATE
	Memory link	:	When his admission was *cancelled*, he started to weep (रो) at the GATE.
	Usage	:	The judge abrogated a law.
29.	Word	:	**Abstinence** (*n*)
	Meaning	:	*resisting from eating and drinking*
	Key	:	ABSENT
	Memory link	:	My uncle remains ABSENT from cocktail party because he *resists* himself *from eating & drinking*.
	Usage	:	*My friend has total abstinence from liquor nowadays.*

30.	Word	:	**Acclaim** (*n*)
	Meaning	:	*prove something energetically and enthusiastically.*
	Key	:	CLAIM
	Memory link	:	He CLAIMED enthusiastically for *proving* 'he was right'
	Usage	:	The book received great critical acclaim.
31.	Word	:	**Accord** (*n*)
	Meaning	:	*agreement*
	Key	:	HYUNDAI ACCORD CAR
	Memory link	:	There was an *agreement* between father and son to buy an HYUNDAI ACCORD CAR.
	Usage	:	A peace accord between two countries.
32.	Word	:	**Acme** (*n*)
	Meaning	:	*Peak; highest point*
	Key	:	LAKME CREAM
	Memory link	:	Last year, LAKME company's sale was at the *peak*.
	Usage	:	Reach at the acme of success.
33.	Word	:	**Acrimonious** (*adj*)
	Meaning	:	*angry and bitter*
	Key	:	A CRY, MONEY
	Memory link	:	He started to CRY when she lost her all MONEY. She became very *angry* and bitter.
	Usage	:	An acrimonious meeting/debate.

34.	Word	:	**Anchorite** (*n*)
	Meaning	:	*a saint.*
	Key	:	ANCHOR (ANCHOR TOOTH-PASTE)
	Memory link	:	*A saint* was cleaning his teeth with ANCHOR toothpaste.
	Usage	:	He is an anchorite.
35.	Word	:	**Alchemy** (*n*)
	Meaning	:	*mediaval chemistry*
	Key	:	ALL CHEMIST
	Memory link	:	ALL CHEMISTS are practising *mediaval* chemistry.
	Usage	:	Practicing and studying alchemy.
36.	Word	:	**Amnesia** (*n*)
	Meaning	:	*loss of memory*
	Key	:	I AM IN नशा
	Memory link	:	The patient says "I am in नशा and as a result *loosing my memory.*"
	Usage	:	An attack of amnesia.
37.	Word	:	**Abate** (*n*)
	Meaning	:	*to reduce; to lessen (of pain, noise, wind)*
	Key	:	WEIGHT,
	Memory link	:	The WEIGHTlifter's muscles were paining so he *reduced* the weights.
	Usage	:	The storm showed no sign of abating.

38.	Word	:	**Accede** (*v*)
	Meaning	:	*to agree*
	Key	:	SEED
	Memory link	:	Every farmer *agreed* with the new variety of SEEDS.
	Usage	:	They will not accede to his demand.
39.	Word	:	**Anathema** (*n*)
	Meaning	:	*a curse*
	Key	:	A THEME
	Memory link	:	A THEMEless script of a movie may be *a curse* for director & producer.
	Usage	:	Public defame is an anathema to me. Racial prejudice is an anathema.
40.	Word	:	**Appal** (*v*)
	Meaning	:	shocked.
	Key	:	A PAL
	Memory link	:	When I saw my best PAL taking bribe, I was *shocked*.
	Usage	:	It appals me to see how big it is!
41.	Word	:	**Baleful** (*adj*)
	Meaning	:	*threatening; deadly*
	Key	:	BAILS (ON CRICKET STUMPS)
	Memory link	:	Both the BAILS fell down from the stumps on the *deadly* ball of Wasim Akram.
	Usage	:	A baleful look.

42.	Word	:	**Bedizen** (*v*)
	Meaning	:	*adorn with showy manner*
	Key	:	KIRAN BEDI – ZEN CAR
	Memory link	:	The ZEN of KIRAN BEDI was adorned with *showy manner* on the Republic day.
	Usage	:	The horses were bedizened before the Republic day.
43.	Word	:	**Belabour** (*v*)
	Meaning	:	to explain excessively
	Key	:	LABOUR
	Memory link	:	The teacher was doing *excessive* LABOUR *to explain* his point.
	Usage	:	I don't want to belabour this point again.
44.	Word	:	**Belittle** (*v*)
	Meaning	:	*To disparage* (नीचा दिखाना)
	Key	:	LITTLE
	Memory link	:	The LITTLE man felt *disparaged* in the party for his small height.
	Usage	:	We should not belittle the poor.
45.	Word	:	**Bellicose** (*adj*)
	Meaning	:	*querrelsome; warlike*
	Key	:	BELLY
	Memory link	:	The *querrelsome* lady was showing her BELLY to the young boys who were teasing her.
	Usage	:	She has bellicose nature.

46.	Word	:	**Blandishment** (*n*)
	Meaning	:	*pleasant talks/action to flatter somebody*
	Key	:	LAND
	Memory link	:	The property dealer who wants to sell his LAND, was flattering the client with his *pleasant talk*.
	Usage	:	He refused to be moved by her blandishment.
47.	Word	:	**Banal** (*adj*)
	Meaning	:	*dull; uninteresting.*
	Key	:	BANNER
	Memory link	:	I don't see BANNERS on road because they are all *dull* & uninteresting.
	Usage	:	Banal remarks/comments in the party.
48.	Word	:	**Bedlam** (*n*)
	Meaning	:	*any place or situation of confusion*
	Key	:	BED, LAMP
	Memory link	:	Who will switch off the LAMP of the BED? this made a *situation of confusion.*
	Usage	:	The children made the room and kitchen absolute bedlam.
49.	Word	:	**Behmoth** (*n*)
	Meaning	:	*a huge animal*
	Key	:	बे मौत
	Memory link	:	एक वहुत बड़ा जानवर बे मौत मारा गया।
	Usage	:	Behmoth in South Africa Jungles.

50.	Word	:	**Brazen** (*adj*)
	Meaning	:	*shameless: bold*
	Key	:	BRA
	Memory link	:	A SHAMLESS lady undressed her shirt and BRA.
	Usage	:	A brazen lady.

TIME : ____________

TEST-2 (25-50) WORDS

I. Write down the key of the following words. For example key for the word Acme Lakme :

Acme	**Lakme**
1. Accord	________
2. Appal	________
3. Bedlam	________
4. Alchemy	________
5. Accede	________
6. Banal	________
7. Amnesia	________
8. Blandishment	________
9. Avarice	________
10. Brazen	________

ANSWERS:

1. Accord car, 2. A Pal, 3. Bed lamp, 4. All chemist, 5. seed, 6. Banner, 7. I am in नशा, 8. land, 9. वारिस, 10. Bra.

II. Tick the right answer of the following words which is closest with the word.

1. Acrimonious
   (a) bitter (b) soft
   (c) understandable (d) enjoying

2. Appaled .
   (a) appeased (b) agreed
   (c) proved (d) shocked

3. Abstinence
   (a) aggrement (b) memorise
   (c) mislead (d) resisting

4. Baleful
   (a) an animal (b) highest
   (c) harmful (d) cancel

5. Abrogate
   (a) to cancel (b) to follow
   (c) to criticize (d) to demand

6. Belabour
   (a) to do hard work (b) to convince
   (c) to flatter (d) to explain excessively

7. Bedizen
   (a) in idol (b) to adorn
   (c) quite (d) beautiful

8. Abate
   (a) to reduce (b) to add
   (c) to calculate (d) to browse

9. Bellicose
   (a) querrelsome (b) loveable
   (c) charismatic (d) healthy some

10. Behemoth
   (a) to speak unnecessarily (b) to visit
   (c) a huge animal (d) confidence

ANSWERS:

1. (a), 2. (d), 3. (d), 4. (c), 5. (a), 6. (d), 7. (b), 8. (a), 9. (a), 10. (c)

III. Write down the meanings of the following words :

S. No.	Word	Meaning
1.	Appease	____________
2.	Brazen	____________
3.	Abrogate	____________
4.	Anathema	____________
5.	Accord	____________
6.	Behemoth	____________
7.	Bedlam	____________
8.	Bellicose	____________
9.	Avarice	____________
10.	Abate	____________

ANSWERS:

1. to lessen, 2. shameless, 3. to cancel, 4. curse, 5. agreement, 6. huge animal, 7. a place of confusion, 8. quarrelsome, 9. greed, 10. to reduce.

IV. Please find out whether the sentences written below are True or False.

1. To belittle a person means to degrade his position. (True/False)
2. During the attack of amnesia, a person looses his memory. (True/False)
3. An anchorite believe in luxury things. (True/False)
4. During the marriage, the horses are bedizened. (True/False)
5. Nobody likes blandishment genuinely. (True/False)
6. In speech banal remarks are very interesting & instructive. (True/False)
7. An drunked person shows total abstinence from liquor. (True/False)
8. Amnesia is related to loss of appetite. (True/False)
9. To say wrong about or National Flag is an anathema. (True/False)
10. When you acclaim something, you try to prove energetically & aggressively. (True/False)

ANSWERS:

1. True, 2. True, 3. False, 4. True, 5. True, 6. False, 7. False, 8. False, 9. True, 10. True.

51.	Word	:	**Bulwark** (*n*)
	Meaning	:	*a defense/protection*
	Key	:	BULL, WALK
	Memory link	:	A furious BULL was WALKING towards me. *To protect* myself I hide in the corner.
	Usage	:	A bulwark against political system.
52.	Word	:	**Bamboozle** (*v*)
	Meaning	:	*to deceive; to cheat*
	Key	:	BAMBOO STICK, जल
	Memory link	:	A wicked saint waved a STICK of BAMBOO tree and sprinkled जल on the people & *cheated* them.
	Usage	:	A Pakistani man bamboozled him of Rs. 500/-
53.	Word	:	**Bandy** (*n*)
	Meaning	:	*discuss lightly*
	Key	:	BAND
	Memory link	:	The musical BAND was very noisy, so we *discussed* the matter very *lightly*.
	Usage	:	The members of the opposition bandied words with each other.
54.	Word	:	**Baroque** (*adj*)
	Meaning	:	*having elaborate and ornamental style in architecture*
	Key	:	BAR
	Memory link	:	This BAR was decorated in an *elaborated and ornamental style*.
	Usage	:	Baroque places.

55.	Word	:	**Beatitude** (*n*)
	Meaning	:	*perfect happiness*
	Key	:	BEAT, ATTITUDE
	Memory link	:	See the ATTITUDE of the students nowadays.The teacher was BEATING them but they were very *happy*.
	Usage	:	Beatitude life.
56.	Word	:	**Bizzare** (*adj*)
	Meaning	:	*very different; unusual*
	Key	:	BAZZAR
	Memory link	:	The BAZZAR was full of *different* & unusal goods.
	Usage	:	This was a bizzare experience of my life.
57.	Word	:	**Beguile** (*v*)
	Meaning	:	*Mislead by cheating or tricking*
	Key	:	गाल
	Memory link	:	In a CHEATING and tricky manner, he kissed on her गाल.
	Usage	:	He beguiled himself by thinking of the old times.
58.	Word	:	**Benison** (*n*)
	Meaning	;	*blessing or good wishes*
	Key	:	बनिए का SON
	Memory link	:	The बनिए का SON has *blessings* or *wishes* that he will earn lot of money.
	Usage	:	The benison of the almighty shall help us through the difficult times.

59.	Word	:	**Besmirch** (*v*)
	Meaning	:	*to damage; to spoil*
	Key	:	मिर्च
	Memory link	:	*To damage* his reputation, we added मिर्च (Red Chilli) in his food/eyes.
	Usage	:	He tried to besmirch his reputation in the party.
60.	Word	:	**Bibulous** (*n*)
	Meaning	:	*A drunkerd person.*
	Key	:	BABULAL
	Memory link	:	BABULAL is a *drunkered person.*
	Usage	:	His idea of a farewell was more than a bibulous gathering.
61.	Word	:	**Blight** (*v*)
	Meaning	:	*To spoil or ruin something*
	Key	:	LIGHT (ELECTRICITY)
	Memory link	:	Our all the efforts on computer became *spoiled.* when the LIGHT went off.
	Usage	:	A career blighted by poor decisions.
62.	Word	:	**Bluster** (*n*)
	Meaning	:	*to speak in a noisy manner*
	Key	:	BLAST
	Memory link	:	After the bomb BLAST, people started *to speak in a noisy manner.*
	Usage	:	It was just bluster. I was not able to understand anything

63.	Word	:	**Bohemian** (*adj*)
	Meaning	:	*unconventional and in artistic way*
	Key	:	बाहें, मियाँ
	Memory link	:	मियाँ जी was meeting everybody in an *unconventional and artistic way* by embracing his बाहें.
	Usage	:	Most creative people live a bohemian life.
64.	Word	:	**Bovine** (*adj*)
	Meaning	:	*slow & stupid*
	Key	:	BOW-WINE
	Memory link	:	A slow and stupid person (बो) the picked up the bow & arrow to hit a wine bottle.
	Usage	:	Bovine person.
65.	Word	:	**Browbeat** (*v*)
	Meaning	:	*to intimidate (डराना)*
	Key	:	BORROW BEAT
	Memory link	:	The recovery department of bank intimidating the people who BORROWED money. They were BEATING the credit holder on the road.
	Usage	:	The senior students were browbeating the new students during the ragging period.
66.	Word	:	**Bumptious** (*adj*)
	Meaning	:	*showing one is very important, arrogant.*
	Key	:	BUMP (उछलना)
	Memory link	:	My *arrogant* friend was BUMPING here and there unnecessarily.
	Usage	:	My boss/teacher has bumptious behaviour.

67.	Word	:	**Bolster** (*v*)
	Meaning	:	*support*
	Key	:	बोल
	Memory link	:	" तू बोल (You speak), I will *support* you" said the father to his son.
	Usage	:	The father bolstered his son's courage and enthusiasm.
68.	Word	:	**Burgeon** (*v*)
	Meaning	:	*to grow very rapidly*
	Key	:	BURGER PAINT
	Memory link	:	Before Diwali, the BURGER PAINT'S sale grew very rapidly.
	Usage	:	A burgreoning talent.
69.	Word	:	**Beleagured** (*adj*)
	Meaning	:	*surrounded by an enemy*
	Key	:	LEAGUE MATCHES
	Memory link	:	In a LEAGUE MATCH of cricket between India and Pakistan, some ememies surounded Indian team.
	Usage	:	A beleagured garrison.
70.	Word	:	**Bout** (*n*)
	Meaning	:	*a short period of intense activity*
	Key	:	OUT
	Memory link	:	After a *short period of intense work* in the school during admission, he was OUT from the school.
	Usage	:	She has bouts of hardwork followed by long period of an illness.

71.	Word	:	**Cabal** (*n*)
	Meaning	:	*a group of people involved in a plot*
	Key	:	कबीला
	Memory link	:	Some कबीले who were *involved in a serious plot* murdered a passer by in the jungle.
	Usage	:	The dictator shot every member of the cabal that had plotted to overthrow him.
72.	Word	:	**Cadence** (*n*)
	Meaning	:	*cat dance*
	Key	:	RHYTHM, BEAT (MUSICAL)
	Memory link	:	On the *musical beat* my CAT started to DANCE.
	Usage	:	Recite poetry with slow cadence.
73.	Word	:	**Cajole** (*v*)
	Meaning	:	*to flatter*
	Key	:	KAJOL ACTRESS
	Memory link	:	Now a days KAJOL is *flattering* Sharukh Khan for getting a role in forthcoming movie.
	Usage	:	She was cajoled into accepting a part in play.
74.	Word	:	**Callow** (*adj*)
	Meaning	:	*immature, inexperienced*
	Key	:	कालू
	Memory link	:	Our servant कालू is still *immature & inexperienced.*
	Usage	:	a callow youth.

75.	Word	:	**Canny** (*adj*)
	Meaning	:	*careful and showing good judgement, esp. in business or spending the money*
	Key	:	PEPSI CAN (Rs. 18/-)
	Memory link	:	He decided to buy two Pepsi bottles instead of PEPSI CANS. He is *very careful in spending the money.*
	Usage	:	a canny fellow.

TIME : ____________

TEST - 3 (50 - 75)

I. Write down the key of the following words. For example: key word for the 'Bandy' is 'Band'.

1. Beguile ________________
2. Benison ________________
3. Bolster ________________
4. Cabal ________________
5. Cajole ________________
6. Canny ________________
7. Capacity ________________
8. Capricious ________________
9. Blight ________________
10. Besmirch ________________
11. Bizzare ________________

ANSWERS:

1. गाल, 2. बनिए का son, 3. बोल, 4. कबीला, 5. Kajol actress, 6. can (Pepsi), 7. capacity, 8. cap, price, 9. light, 10. मिर्च (chilly), 11. Bazzar.

II. Below, a word follows one exact word of similar meaning. Try to locate the word :

1. Bandy
   (a) discussion (b) confusion
   (c) music (d) understandable

2. Bamboozle
   (a) to encourage (b) to decieve
   (c) to criticize (d) to discuss

3. Callow
   (a) immature (b) experienced
   (c) protection (d) dispute

4. Cabal
   (a) speak
   (b) boss
   (c) flatter
   (d) a group of people distinctively

5. Bibulous

(a) confused (b) changeable

(c) a drunkard (d) cheat person

6. Blight

(a) light (b) a disease

(c) increase (d) understanding

7. Besmirch

(a) to spoil (b) to reward

(c) to imagine (d) to create

8. Beatitude

(a) happiness (b) curse

(c) sudden (d) flatter

9. Bizzare

(a) feeling of disappointment

(b) unusual

(c) principle

(d) explaination disappointment beat

10. Bension

(a) a wise man (b) support

(c) blessing (d) a short period

ANSWERS:

1. (a), 2. (b), 3. (a). 4. (d), 5. (c), 6. (b), 7. (a), 8. (a), 9. (b), 10. (c)

III. Match the following :

1. Cajole	(a) increasing
2. Burgeoning	(b) arrogant
3. Bohemian	(c) unconventional & artistic
4. Bumptious	(d) to cheat
5. Beguile	(e) noisy
6. Bluster	(f) a short period
7. Belegured	(g) careful & good judgement
8. Bout	(h) surrounded

9. Canny	(i) to flatter
10. Bizzare	(j) very different

ANSWERS:

1. (i), 2. (a), 3. (c), 4. (b), 5. (d), 6. (e), 7. (h), 8. (f), 9. (g), 10. (j)

IV. Some of the following statements are *false*, others are *true* check the correct response.

1. When somebody *bamboozles* the other person it mean he decieves him. (True/False)
2. A callow person is an experienced person. (True/False)
3. When we criticize somebody in public we try to besmirch his/her reputation (True/False)
4. We should not browbeat the children unnecessarily. (True/False)
5. Thinking of big plans but not doing anything is a case of beguiling oneself. (True/False)
6. A fatal accident may blight your career. (True/False)
7. Parents should bolster their children. (True/False)
8. A bibulous person abstains from liquor. (True/False)
9. Some authors/poets write in a bohemian style. (True/False)
10. Beatitude means feeling sad. (True/False)

ANSWERS:

1. True, 2. False, 3. True, 4. True, 5. True, 6. True, 7. True, 8. False, 9. True, 10. False.

76.	Word	:	**Canvass** (*v*)
	Meaning	:	*asking for vote*
	Key	:	CANE-ASS
	Memory link	:	Some politicans sitting on ASS with CANE in their hand were asking for votes in our colony.
	Usage	:	canvassing the constituency next month.
77.	Word	:	**Capacious** (*adj*)
	Meaning	:	*roomy*
	Key	:	CAPACITY
	Memory link	:	The CAPACITY of my drawing room is very good. 15 people can sit together comfortably. This is very *roomy*.
	Usage	:	A capacious boot of car.
78.	Word	:	**Capricious** (*adj*)
	Meaning	:	*showing sudden changes*
	Key	:	CAP PRICE
	Memory link	:	As the PRICE of CAP was *suddenly changing*, we bought it quickly.
	Usage	:	A capricous climate.
79.	Word	:	**Cardinal** (*adj*)
	Meaning	:	*principal, chief, most important*
	Key	:	CARD
	Memory link	:	Visa CARD is *most important* for visiting a foreign country.
	Usage	:	A cardinal rule/reason.

80:	Word	:	**Careen** (*v*)
	Meaning	:	*sway from side to side*
	Key	:	करीना कपूर (Actress)
	Memory link	:	I saw *Kareena Kapoor* in the movie swaying her waist *from one side to another.*
	Usage	:	Car careening down the hill.
81.	Word	:	**Carnage** (*n*)
	Meaning	:	*killing many people*
	Key	:	CAR
	Memory link	:	Millitants *killed many people* in Sri Nagar & ran away in the CAR.
	Usage	:	A scene of carnage.
82.	Word	:	**Cataclysm** (*adj*)
	Meaning	:	*any sudden, violent, change esp flood, eathquake*
	Key	:	CAT-KILL
	Memory link	:	Lot of CAT got KILLED because of *sudden violent change esp flood, earthyoate.*
	Usage	:	The cataclysmic events of war.
83.	Word	:	**Celerity** (*n*)
	Meaning	:	*speedily*
	Key	:	CELEBRITY
	Memory link	:	Crowd appreriated the CELEBRITY for his ability to give autograph *speedily.*
	Usage	:	With a great clearity, he ran away.

84.	Word	:	**Censure** (*v*)
	Meaning	:	*to disapprove, to condemn as wrong*
	Key	:	Censor board
	Memory link	:	Initially CENSOR BOARD *disapproved* Bandit Queen movie.
	Usage	:	This is highly controversial. Censure it immediately.
85.	Word	:	**Certitude** (*n*)
	Meaning	:	*a feeling of sureness*
	Key	:	CERTIFICATE
	Memory link	:	CERTIFICATES or documents gives the *feeling of sureness* to the employers.
	Usage	:	I like his certitude of giving answers.
86.	Word	:	**Chagrin** (*n*)
	Meaning	:	*feeling disappointment due to mistake*
	Key	:	चाय गिरी (Tea fell on clothes)
	Memory link	:	Waiter से चाय गिरी and he felt *disappointed due to his mistake*.
	Usage	:	Much of his chargin, he came last in race.
87.	Word	:	**Chequered** (*adj*)
	Meaning	:	*period of good and bad time*
	Key	:	CHEQUES
	Memory link	:	"Whether my son is in *good* or *bad time*, he never forgets to send me CHEQUES" said the old lady.
	Usage	:	A chequered career.

88.	Word	:	**Chimerical** (*adj*)
	Meaning	:	*fantastic; highly imaginative*
	Key	:	SHE MARRY कल
	Memory link	:	"SHE will MARRY me tomarrow (कल)" — whet a *fantastic idea!*
	Usage	:	A chimerical notion/claim.
89.	Word	:	**Cipher** (*n*)
	Meaning	:	*secret code*
	Key	:	(सिफर) उर्दू का शब्द ZERO के लिए
	Memory link	:	His briefcase, opening *secret code* is CIPHER (0).
	Usage	:	The messages were sent to the agent to USA in ciphers.
90.	Word	:	**Circuitous** (*adj*)
	Meaning	:	*roundabout* (घुमावदार)
	Key	:	Circus
	Memory link	:	The auto-rickshaw driver took us to the CIRCUS through *roundabout* route.
	Usage	:	A circuitous route.
91.	Word	:	**Circumspect** (*adj*)
	Meaning	:	*cautious*
	Key	:	SIR-COME-SPECS
	Memory link	:	SIR is keeping the SPECS *continously* since it is very costly.
	Usage	:	Having a circumspect approach during election.

92.	Word	:	**Clairvoyance** (*n*)
	Meaning	:	*keen ability to grasp things*
	Key	:	CLEAR VOICE
	Memory link	:	The speaker's VOICE was very CLEAR so I was able to *grasp many things* with ease.
	Usage	:	Show clairvoyance in computer field.
93.	Word	:	**Cliche** (*n*)
	Meaning	:	*phrase repeatitively used*
	Key	:	CLUTCH
	Memory link	:	Avoid using phrase in the speech *repeatitively* like CLUTCH in an automobile.
	Usage	:	Don't use cliche in your speech.
94.	Word	:	**Cogent** (*adj*)
	Meaning	:	*convincing*
	Key	:	CO-COMPANY, AGENT
	Memory link	:	Nestle company's AGENT was very *convincing*.
	Usage	:	He produced cogent reasons for change in policy.
95.	Word	:	**Coerce** (*v*)
	Meaning	:	to *compel; to force.*
	Key	:	COURSE
	Memory link	:	My father *compelled* me to do the computer COURSE.
	Usage	:	Don't coerce me for marriage.

96.	Word	:	**Compendium** (*n*)
	Meaning	:	*brief summary*
	Key	:	कम – PEN
	Memory link	:	कम Pen use करके *brief summary* लिखो।
	Usage	:	This book is an invaluable compendium of my ideas and experiences.
97.	Word	:	**Conflagration** (*n*)
	Meaning	:	*A wild fire*
	Key	:	FLAG
	Memory link	:	National FLAG caught *wild fire* on Independence Day.
	Usage	:	A conflagration during the war.
98.	Word	:	**Copious** (*adj*)
	Meaning	:	*plenty, too much*
	Key	:	COPY
	Memory link	:	*Plenty* of COPIES of this book are available in the library.
	Usage	:	Copious flowers/tears.
99.	Word	:	**Covert** (*adj*)
	Meaning	:	*secret, hidden*
	Key	:	COVER
	Memory link	:	He wrapped the *secret* file in a COVER handed over to the CBI.
	Usage	:	He had covert idea in the mind.

100.	Word	:	**Credulous** (*adj*)
	Meaning	:	*believable*
	Key	:	CREDIT
	Memory link	:	He is a belivable fellow, you can give him CREDIT as much as he wants.
	Usage	:	He is a credulous person.

TIME : ____________

TEST - 4 (75 - 100)

I. Write down the keys of following words.

S. No.	Word	Keys
	Covert	Cover
1.	Certitude	______
2.	Chagrin	______
3.	Cipher	______
4.	Cogent	______
5.	Copious	______
6.	Clairvoyance	______
7.	Credulous	______
8.	Conflagration	______
9.	Cardinal	______
10.	Chequered	______
11.	Chimerical	______
12.	Carnage	______
13.	Coerce	______
14.	Compendium	______
15.	Celerity	______

ANSWERS:

1. Certificate, 2. चाय गिरी, 3. सिफर, 4. Company-Agent, 5. Copy 6. Clear voice, 7. Credit, 8. Flag, 9. Card, 10. Cheque 11. She marry,कल 12. Car, 13. Course; 14. कम Pen, 15. Celebrity.

II. Please Tick the right answer of the following :

1. Circumspect
   (a) summary (b) cautious
   (c) careless (d) follow

2. Cliche
   (a) respective (b) sudden
   (c) attack (d) used phrase/word repeatitively

3. Conflagration
   (a) remuneration (b) astute
   (c) baleful (d) a wild fire

4. Censure
   (a) to perceive (b) to stop
   (c) to move (d) to humiliate

5. Careen
   (a) sway from (b) to flatter
   (c) short stay (d) rigidness one to another

6. Canvass
   (a) a kind of cloth (b) to say slowly
   (c) asking vote (d) visiting

7. Cataclysm
   (a) stationary (b) sudden
   (c) creative (d) gradual

8. Capricious
   (a) changeable (b) constant
   (c) mad (d) stubborn

9. Capacious
   (a) beguile (b) enjoyable
   (c) condemn (d) roomy

10. Chequered
   (a) check (b) ups & down
   (c) stammered (d) shouted

ANSWERS:

1. (b), 2. (a), 3. (d), 4. (b), 5. (a), 6. (c), 7. (b), 8. (a), 9. (d), 10. (b)

III. Now test your increasing understanding of these 10 words by marking each of the following statements "True" or "False" :

1. Increasing population is a cardinal problem of India. (True/False)
2. A chequered career means period of good time in the life. (True/False)

3. One day I shall become like Bill Grates and buy USA— it is a chimerical notion. (True/False)
4. Cabal means a small group of people. (True/False)
5. Capricious people always achieve success and are very persistent. (True/False)
6. When tyre get punctured, car starts careening. (True/False)
7. Use cliches in your language — it makes the language interesting. (True/False)
8. A marketing agent need not to be cogent. (True/False)
9. Compendium means a detailed summary. (True/False)
10. 'Clairvoyance' is a good characteristic of successful people. (True/False)

ANSWERS:

1. False, 2. False, 3. True, 4. True, 5. False, 6. True, 7. False, 8. False, 9. False, 10. True.

IV. By now you have developed real and assured control over these words. Therefore you will be able to sail through the next exercise with the greatest of ease and a perfect score. Mark the right answer :

1. There was a *chagrin* on his face
   (a) shining
   (b) disappointment
   (c) happiness

2. *Cataclysmic* attack means
   (a) very harmful
   (b) sudden
   (c) defensive

3. *Cipher* means
   (a) a secret code
   (b) a kind of juice
   (c) a discussion

4. With a great *celerity*, he ran away
   (a) happiness
   (b) anxiety
   (c) quickness

5. Who can *coerce* you to leave this job?
   (a) force
   (b) discourage
   (c) suggest

6. The policeman were *circumspecting* during the curfew period
   (a) on move
   (b) cautious & alert
   (c) announcing

7. The book is a *compendium* of ideas
   (a) a detailed explaisation
   (b) a brief summary
   (c) critical explanation

8. A *conflagration* during war
   (a) a wild fire
   (b) an announcement
   (c) an relief operation

9. A *covert* plan
   (a) appropriate
   (b) open
   (c) secret

10. *Copious* tears rolled down from her eyes
    (a) plenty
    (b) hot
    (c) some

ANSWERS:

1. (b), 2. (b), 3. (a), 4. (c), 5. (a), 6. (b), 7. (b), 8. (a), 9. (c), 10. (a)

101.	Word	:	**Culinary** (*adj*)
	Meaning	:	*related to kitchen/cooking*
	Key	:	CLEAN
	Memory link	:	CLEANLINESS is essential in the *kitchen*/cooking.
	Usage	:	A culinary job.
102.	Word	:	**Cull** (*v*)
	Meaning	:	to reject
	Key	:	कल
	Memory link	:	If you come कल (tomarow), you'll *be rejected.*
	Usage	:	He culls various plans & selects only the best.
103.	Word	:	**Culpable** (*adj*)
	Meaning	:	*blame worty, deserving blame.*
	Key	:	CULPRIT
	Memory link	:	This CULPRIT *deserves blame* & must be punished severly.
	Usage	:	Culpable fellow/issue.
104.	Word	:	**Cynosure** (*n*)
	Meaning	:	*a centre of attention or interest*
	Key	:	DINOSAUR
	Memory link	:	DINOSAUR was the *centre of attention* in Stephen Spillberg's Jurrasik Park movie.
	Usage	:	She was cynosure in the party/movie.

105.	Word	:	**Calumny** (*n*)
	Meaning	:	*a false statement to defame somebody*
	Key	:	COLOUMN (IN NEWSPAPER)
	Memory link	:	*A false statement* was deliberately published in the main COLOUMN of the 'The Times of India' *to defame congress.*
	Usage	:	A victim of vicious calumnies.
106.	Word	:	**Candid** (*adj*)
	Meaning	:	*honest*
	Key	:	CANDY
	Memory link	:	The shopkeeper unknowingly gave an extra CANDY but the child was *honest* enough to return it.
	Usage	:	He gave candid view on this topic.
107.	Word	:	**Captious** (*adj*)
	Meaning	:	*quick to find fault*
	Key	:	CAP
	Memory link	:	She could not decide the colour of cap. In every CAP, she would *find a fault* quickly.
	Usage	:	Captious boss/person.
108.	Word	:	**Carp** (*v*)
	Meaning	:	*to complain continually about unimportant matters and finding faults*
	Key	:	CAR (old)
	Memory link	:	The mechanic was *continually complaining about* the minor rectification of my *old car*.
	Usage	:	Have a carping tongue.

109.	Word	:	**Cartographer** (*n*)
	Meaning	:	*map-maker*
	Key	:	CARTOON-GRAPHIC-DESIGN
	Memory link	:	A *map maker* was designing CARTOONS of politicians a GRAPH paper.
	Usage	:	He is a cartographer. designs very good map of any territory.
110.	Word	:	**Cathartic** (*adj*)
	Meaning	:	*purgative; that causes bowels to empty; the process of releasing strong feeling (anger, hate)*
	Key	:	कत्था (पान में)
	Memory link	:	The Pan-Wala added too much कत्था, which was very PURGATIVE. The whole night I had to sit in toilet.
	Usage	:	This drug is cathartic in nature.
111.	Word	:	**Caveat** (*n*)
	Meaning	:	*wheat (in storeroom)*
	Key	:	warning
	Memory link	:	Food Corporation of India issued a *warning* to the food inspector for poor storage of WHEAT.
	Usage	:	I recommended the deal but with some caveats.
112.	Word	:	**Charlatan** (*n*)
	Meaning	:	*a person who claims more knowledge/ skill than he was has*
	Key	:	चार – ten
	Memory link	:	Ramvir has studied upto class but he claims TENTH. He *claims more knowledge than he has.*
	Usage	:	Flush of charlatan doctors in the city.

113.	Word	:	**Cherubic** (*adj*)
	Meaning	:	*with a round innocent face*
	Key	:	चारु (a name)
	Memory link	:	My sister's newly born son. NAMED चारु has *round innocent face*.
	Usage	:	Cherubic child.
114.	Word	:	**Cogitate** (*v*)
	Meaning	:	*meditate; to think deeply*
	Key	:	COCK-IT-ATE
	Memory link	:	IT is that COCK which *meditates* after EATING.
	Usage	:	My mother was cogitating on this issue.
115.	Word	:	**Commiserate** (*v*)
	Meaning	:	*to sympathhise; show pity for*
	Key	:	POLICE COMMISSIONER
	Memory link	:	The POLICE COMMISSIONER sympathised with the pick-pocketers & allowed them to go.
	Usage	:	I commiserated with her on the death of her son.
116.	Word	:	**Conjecture** (*n*)
	Meaning	:	*a guess*
	Key	:	JACK (OF PLAYING CARDS)
	Memory link	:	I wrongly *guessed* that my opponent had JACK of Spade.
	Usage	:	We must not come to the conclusions on the basis of conjectures.

117.	Word	:	**Contagious** (*adj*)
	Meaning	:	*spreads through touching*
	Key	:	CONTACT
	Memory link	:	Infectious diseases *spread through* air CONTACT.
	Usage	:	Contagious circles or contagious disease.
118.	Word	:	**Coroborate** (*adj*)
	Meaning	:	*to give support to a statement, belief, theory.*
	Key	:	COLLOBORATE
	Memory link	:	Yamha company of Japan gave technical *suport* to Escorts Ltd. India under COLLOBORATION with Escorts Yamaha India Ltd.
	Usage	:	Corroborative reports for the project.
119.	Word	:	**Cupidity** (*n*)
	Meaning	:	*strong desire for wealth*
	Key	:	QUEUE-PEOPLE
	Memory link	:	PEOPLE standing in a queue for long hours are having strong desire for wealth.
	Usage	:	His cupidity lead him to disaster.
120.	Word	:	**Curry** (*v*)
	Meaning	:	*seek favour*
	Key	:	CHICKEN CURRY
	Memory link	:	He was a selfish businessman. To *seek favour* he invited the clients to a chicken CURRY party.
	Usage	:	The helpers curried favour from the manager.

121.	Word	:	**Chary** (*adj*)
	Meaning	:	*cautious*
	Key	:	CHERRY
	Memory link	:	Be *cautions* while polishing your shoes with CHERRY polish.
	Usage	:	Chary of Lending money.
122.	Word	:	**Colander** (*n*)
	Meaning	:	*a special utensil*
	Key	:	CALENDER
	Memory link	:	A shopkeeper gave a free CALENDER alongwith *a special utesil* on Diwali.
	Usage	:	The woman used the colander to strain the tea leaves.
123.	Word	:	**Cower** (*v*)
	Meaning	:	*shrink as from fear*
	Key	:	COW
	Memory link	:	When the cow saw the lion, she *shrank out of fear*.
	Usage	:	The child cowerd in one corner when her mother scolded him.
124.	Word	:	**Cursory** (*adj*)
	Meaning	:	*hastily done*
	Key	:	CURSOR (IN A COMPUTER)
	Memory link	:	Don't move CURSOR so *hastily*. The computer will stop functioning.
	Usage	:	He gave a cursory look on the newspaper.

125.	Word	:	**Condescend** (*v*)
	Meaning	:	*to comedown voluntarily*
	Key	:	DESCEND
	Memory link	:	The boss DESCENDED from the top floor VOLUNTARILY & started to shake hands with junior staff.
	Usage	:	He would not condescend with junior staff.

TIME : ___________

TEST - 5 (101-125)

I. Write down the keys of following words :

Culpable	**Culprit**
1. Candid	____________
2. Cursory	____________
3. Cynosure	____________
4. Cogitate	____________
5. Carping	____________
6. Calumny	____________
7. Caveat	____________
8. Cherubic	____________
9. Colander	____________
10. Commiserate	____________
11. Conjecture	____________
12. Curry	____________
13. Charry	____________
14. Cartographer	____________
15. Culinary	____________

ANSWERS:

1. Candy, 2. Cursor, 3. Dinasour, 4. Cuk-it-ate, 5. car (old) 6. column (Newspaper), 7. Wheat, 8. Charu, 9. Calender, 10. Commisoner, 11. Jeck, 12. (chicken) curry, 13. Cherry polish, 14. Cartoon graph, 15. clean

II. Match the follwing :

1. Chary	(a) a person having less knoweldge but claims more
2. Commiserate	(b) greedy
3. Charlatan	(c) to sympathize
4. Carp	(d) quick to find fault
5. Captious	(e) support
6. Cynosure	(f) cautions
7. Candid	(g) touching
8. Corroborate	(h) honest & frank

9. Contagious (i) centre of attention
10. Cupidity (j) to complain unnecessarily

ANSWERS:

1. (f), 2. (c), 3. (a), 4. (j), 5. (d), 6. (i), 7. (h), 8. (e), 9. (g), 10. (b)

III. Tick the right synonym of the given 10 words :

1. Caveat
   (a) understanding (b) lovely
   (c) warning (d) disguise

2. Candid
   (a) confident (b) open & frank
   (c) sorrow (d) hostility

3. Conjecture
   (a) to criticize (b) believable
   (c) refill (d) a guess

4. Colander
   (a) an utensil (b) short
   (c) wealth (d) abundance

5. Contagious
   (a) spread through touch (b) closed
   (c) cautious (d) indirect

6. Cull
   (a) to leave (b) to reject
   (c) to shed (d) to sway

7. Catharsis
   (a) a disease (b) opportunity
   (c) purgative (d) critical

8. Captious
   (a) find fault (b) pretending
   (c) artificial (d) disguise

9. Cherubic
   (a) Innocent (b) speedily
   (c) round face (d) to condemn

10. Cogitate
   (a) to weep (b) to meditate
   (c) to suggest (d) to apply

ANSWERS:

1. (c), 2. (b), 3. (d), 4. (a), 5. (a), 6. (b), 7. (c), 8. (a), 9. (c), 10. (b)

IV. Check the following statements and find out whether they are "true" or "false".

1. Corrupt people have covert ideas in their mind. (True/False)
2. Cull means to accept the things happily. (True/False)
3. Cynosure means centre of attention. (True/False)
4. A culinary job is related to office work. (True/False)
5. Generally old & dogmatic women have carping nature. (True/False)
6. Cupidity means greed for money. (True/False)
7. Yawning is contagious. (True/False)
8. We should try to commiserate with weaker section of the society. (True/False)
9. The culpable persons should be punished. (True/False)
10. Credulous people are liked by everybody. (True/False)

ANSWERS:

1. True, 2. False, 3. True, 4. False, 5. True, 6. True, 7. True, 8. True, 9. True, 10. True.

126.	Word	:	**Cache** (*n*)
	Meaning	:	*secret place*
	Key	:	CASH
	Memory link	:	You should put this jewellery & CASH in a *secret place*.
	Usage	:	An arm cache.
127.	Word	:	**Canon** (*n*)
	Meaning	:	*a basic law or principle*
	Key	:	CANON CAMERA
	Memory link	:	The photographer put out a CANON camera from his bag and told the *basic principle* of photography to the students of photography club.
	Usage	:	Canons of tribal group are very strict.
128.	Word	:	**Cantankerous** (*adj*)
	Meaning	:	*bad tempered*
	Key	:	TANKER,
	Memory link	:	In film Border, Sunny Deol became *bad tempered* when Sunil Shetty was not moving the TANKER ahead.
	Usage	:	He is a cantankerous person. Nobody would like to talk to him.
129.	Word	:	**Chaff** (*n*)
	Meaning	:	*worthless*
	Key	:	CHEF
	Memory link	:	Our newly appointed CHEF is *worthless* person. He doesn't know even how to prepare Tomato Soup.
	Usage	:	One should learn to seperate the chaff from the main contents before presenting anything.

130.	Word	:	**Choleric** (*adj*)
	Meaning	:	*easily made angry*
	Key	:	CHOLERA (हैज़ा)
	Memory link	:	He was a nice man. But after CHOLERA, his nature has been changed.
	Usage	:	A choleric old man.
131.	Word	:	**Concomitant** (*adj*)
	Meaning	:	*happening at the same time*
	Key	:	COMMITMENT
	Memory link	:	We made a COMMITMENT that our *action will start at the same time.*
	Usage	:	She enjoyed travelling and all its concomitant discomforts.
132.	Word	:	**Conjugal** (*adj*)
	Meaning	:	*of relation between husband & wife*
	Key	:	जुगल जोड़ी
	Memory link	:	This *husband-wife* (जुगल जोड़ी) is god-created.
	Usage	:	Conjugal discussion.
133.	Word	:	**Culmination** (*n*)
	Meaning	:	*attainment of highest point*
	Key	:	कल-ME-NATION
	Memory link	:	कल मैं will attain great *height of* success to serve MY NATION.
	Usage	:	The fight between USA & Afghanistan was a culmination of all.

134.	Word	:	**Crabbed** (*adj*)
	Meaning	:	*peevish; irritating*
	Key	:	CRAB (केकड़ा)
	Memory link	:	My neighbour behaves like a CRAB. He is *peevish & irritating* on the street children.
	Usage	:	The crabbed old man was avoided by all the children.
135.	Word	:	**Cryptic** (*adj*)
	Meaning	:	*secret*
	Key	:	CREEP
	Memory link	:	The cat was trying to CREEP *secretly* towards the child.
	Usage	:	I cannot understand the cryptic plans in his mind.
136.	Word	:	**Cul-de-sac** (*n*)
	Meaning	:	*trap*
	Key	:	कल-SACK
	Memory link	:	कल one employee was *trapped* redhanded doing some mischief so he was SACKED from the job.
	Usage	:	The particular brand of Socialism had entered a cul-de-sac.
137.	Word	:	**Carmine** (*adj*)
	Meaning	:	*red purplish colour*
	Key	:	MY CAR
	Memory link	:	MY CAR is of *red-purplish colour*.
	Usage	:	My girlfriend like carmine flowers.

138.	Word	: **Cognomen** (*n*)
	Meaning	: *last name, surname*
	Key	: CONGRESS-MEN
	Memory link	: A notice was issued that all CONGRESS-MEN will write their names with their *surnames* like this way : Sonia Gandhi Cognomen Madav Rao Schidhia Cognomen
	Usage	: What is your cognomen?
139.	Word	: **Digress** (*v*)
	Meaning	: *to leave the main subject / work*
	Key	: GRASS
	Memory link	: The gardners who was cutting the GRASS *left his work* when he saw a beautiful girl passing by the garden.
	Usage	: The speaker digressed from the topic during his presentation.
140.	Word	: **Diligence** (*n*)
	Meaning	: *careful; hardworking*
	Key	: DELHI – GENTS
	Memory link	: The GENTS OF DELHI are very *careful & hardworking.*
	Usage	: She shows great diligence in her school work.
141.	Word	: **Dipsomaniac** (*n*)
	Meaning	: *one who has a great desire for liquor*
	Key	: DIP SO MAN
	Memory link	: Our WATCHMAN has a *great desire for liquor* & wants to DIP SO deeply in the liquor.
	Usage	: Dipsomaniacs drink too much liquor.

142.	Word	:	**Disavowal** (*n*)
	Meaning	:	*denial; to say that something is not true*
	Key	:	VOWELS (a,e,i,o,u)
	Memory link	:	The english teacher *denied* the students that she never said that students would put VOWEL 'a' before word 'honest'.
	Usage	:	Disavowal against women Reservation Bill.
143.	Word	:	**Disconcert** (*v*)
	Meaning	:	*to confuse; to upset*
	Key	:	THIS CONCERT
	Memory link	:	*To upset* everybody in THIS musical CONCERT, I disconnected the electrical supply.
	Usage	:	She has the disconcerting habit of addressing younger women.
144.	Word	:	**Discord** (*n*)
	Meaning	:	*quarrel, disagreement*
	Key	:	THIS CORD
	Memory link	:	Instruction was given that those who will *quarrel* will be tied with THIS CORD.
	Usage	:	A note of discord crept into their relationship.
145.	Word	:	**Discursive** (*adj*)
	Meaning	:	*changing from one topic to another*
	Key	:	CURSIVE WRITING
	Memory link	:	Since you are *changing from one topic to another* write the later topic in CURSIVE WRITING so that you can distinguish it from the former.
	Usage	:	The play was very discursive in style. Very few people could understand the story.

146.	Word	:	**Disinterested** *(adj)*
	Meaning	:	*not influenced by personal feeling or interest; unbiased*
	Key	:	NOT INERESTED
	Memory link	:	The judge didn't take any INTEREST whether the accused was his neighbour or not & gave *unbiased* decision.
	Usage	:	My advice is completely disinterested.
147.	Word	:	**Diurnal** (*adj*)
	Meaning	:	*day time*
	Key	:	DAIRY-A-नल
	Memory link	:	He was running his diary under the नल during day time.
	Usage	:	The diurnal rotation of the earth.
148.	Word	:	**Dicey** (*adj*)
	Meaning	:	*risky; uncertain*
	Key	:	DICE
	Memory link	:	The result is always *uncertain* when you play with a DICE.
	Usage	:	A dicey situation for getting the money.
149.	Word	:	**Deadpan** (*adj*)
	Meaning	:	*wooden; uninteresting*
	Key	:	PAN, DEAD
	Memory link	:	A *wooden* PAN is almost a deadpan because we cannot put it on fire.
	Usage	:	It was a deadpan comedy-quite uninteresting.

150.	Word	:	**Dirge** (*n*)
	Meaning	:	*a song, poem of grief*
	Key	:	डर (फिल्म)
	Memory link	:	I was listening *sad song* of डर फिल्म — "जादू तेरी नजर खुशबू तेरा बदन..."
	Usage	:	The dirge brought tears in eyes of my girl freind.

TIME : ____________

TEST - 6 (126- 150)

I. Write down the key words of the following word :

Word	Key
1. Cache	________________
2. Dirge	________________
3. Chaff	________________
4. Crabbed	________________
5. Cognomen	________________
6. Culmination	________________
7. Dogmatic	________________
8. Discursive	________________
9. Cryptic	________________
10. Dipsomaniac	________________
11. Diligence	________________
12. Diurnal	________________
13. Disconcert	________________
14. Canon	________________
15. Digress	________________

ANSWER:

1. Cash, 2. डर (Movie), 3. Chef, 4. Crab, 5. Congressness, 6. कल- Me-Nation, 7. Dog, 8. Cursive writing, 9. Grip, 10. Dip, so, 11. Delhi, gents, 12. Dairy नल, 13. This concert, 14. Canon Camera, 15. जुगल जोड़ी

II. Match the following with appropriate word.

1. Disconcert	(a) day time
2. Diurnal	(b) to deny
3. Disavowal	(c) uninteresting & inactive
4. Cul-de-sack	(d) happening same time
5. Deadpan	(e) to upset
6. Cache	(f) risky
7. Dicey	(g) angry
8. Choleric	(h) to trap

9. Concomitant (i) hidden
10. Discord (j) disagreement

ANSWERS:

1. (e), 2. (a), 3. (b), 4. (h), 5. (c), 6. (i), 7. (f), 8. (g), 9. (d), 10. (j)

III. Tick the correct answer of the *italicized* word.

1. *Cantankerous* person means
   (a) story
   (b) bad tempered
   (c) arrogant

2. *Conjugal* discussion
   (a) related to husband and wife
   (b) showy
   (c) brief

3. *Culmination* of all the knowledge
   (a) lowest point
   (b) collection
   (c) highest point

4. *A choleric* old women
   (a) easily angry women
   (b) dogmatic
   (c) weak

5. I became *disconcerted* during the interview
   (a) excited
   (b) confused
   (c) thrilled

6. I like *carmine* flowers
   (a) a kind of flowers
   (b) red purplish colour
   (c) a bunch

7. The play was *discursive* in the style
   (a) changing from one to another
   (b) interesting
   (c) dull

8. *Disinterested* means
   (a) not interested
   (b) deviatied
   (c) biased & prejudiced

9. People of villages are really *diligent.*
   (a) careless
   (b) hardworking
   (c) ambitious

10. A deadpan comedy means
    (a) interesting
    (b) uninteresting & boring
    (c) fast

ANSWERS:

1. (b), 2. (a), 3. (c), 4. (a), 5. (b), 6. (b), 7. (a), 8. (c), 9. (b), 10. (b)

IV. Write down the meaning of 10 important words given below:

1. Canon ____________________
2. Disavowel ____________________
3. Digress ____________________
4. Cryptic ____________________
5. Condescend ____________________
6. Dicey ____________________
7. Disinterested ____________________
8. Dipsomaniac ____________________
9. Diligent ____________________
10. Conjugal ____________________

ANSWERS:

1. A principle or law; 2. Denial; 3. Go away from main topic 4. Secret, 5. To come down, 6. Risky & uncertain, 7. Unbiased, 8. Who has great desire for liquor, 9. Hardworking, 10. Related to marriage

151.	Word	:	**Distrain** (*n*)
	Meaning	:	*the act of to seizing goods for debt*
	Key	:	THIS TRAIN
	Memory link	:	The police *seized the goods* from the passanger of THIS TRAIN.
	Usage	:	The shopkeeper imposed distrain on poor man for not paying interest.
152.	Word	:	**Dotage** (*n*)
	Meaning	:	*childish state due to old age*
	Key	:	DOT – AGE
	Memory link	:	Due to old AGE, my grand father starts behaving *childishly*. He was doing nothing but putting DOTS continuously.
	Usage	:	The old man became dotage in 70's.
153.	Word	:	**Dyspepsia** (*n*)
	Meaning	:	*pain due to indigetion*
	Key	:	PEPSI
	Memory link	:	I was feeling *pain due to indigetion.* My friend advised me to take PEPSI.
	Usage	:	Feel dyspeptic after the meal.
154.	Word	:	**Deranged** (*adj*)
	Meaning	:	insane; stupid.
	Key	:	MOUNTAIN RANGE, RANGER CYCLE
	Memory link	:	My friend has become *stupid*. He is going to MOUNTAIN RANGES on RANGER CYCLE.
	Usage	:	She has become completely deranged.

155.	Word	:	**Deride** (*v*)
	Meaning	:	*to ridicule*
	Key	:	RIDE
	Memory link	:	A handicap person was trying to RIDE the horse & fell down. My daughter laughed at him. I *ridiculed* at her for this act.
	Usage	:	They derided her efforts.
156.	Word	:	**Descant** (*v*)
	Meaning	:	*discuss in detail*
	Key	:	DESK ANT
	Memory link	:	An ANT sitting on DESK was *dicussing in detail* about her marriage with her friend.
	Usage	:	He would descant before passing any judgement.
157.	Word	:	**Diaphanous** (*adj*)
	Meaning	:	*transparent*
	Key	:	DIAL, PHONE
	Memory link	:	An enormous size *transparent* PHONE was designed by an Japanese company for the exhibition. This phone can be checked by DIALING.
	Usage	:	A diaphanous door
158.	Word	:	**Dilletente** (*adj*)
	Meaning	:	*one who is not an expert*
	Key	:	ढीली (LOOSE) TENT
	Memory link	:	"यह TENT बहुत ढीली बंधी है। I think you are *not an expert in this*" said my father to the worker.
	Usage	:	He is a dilletente person.

159.	Word	:	**Disport** (*v*)
	Meaning	:	*to smile*
	Key	:	THIS PORT (AIRPORT)
	Memory link	:	When I saw her at THIS PORT, She *smiled* at me.
	Usage	:	The clients disported themselves at the stage show.
160.	Word	:	**Dregs** (*n*)
	Meaning	:	*worthless things*
	Key	:	DRUGS
	Memory link	:	DRUGS are the *worthless things*.
	Usage	:	Please dump this where rest of the dregs have been dumped.
161.	Word	:	**Dubious** (*adj*)
	Meaning	:	*doubtful*
	Key	:	डूबी
	Memory link	:	I am *doubtful* – शायद मेरी friend डूब गई है।
	Usage	:	His background is little dubious.
162.	Word	:	**Dulcet** (*adj*)
	Meaning	:	*sweet Sounding*
	Key	:	DULL SET (STAGE)
	Memory link	:	The SET of stage was looking very DULL. So I decided to go. Suddenly I heard a *sweet sound* of a girl from the stage.
	Usage	:	I thought I recognized your dulcet tone.

163.	Word	:	**Defalcate** (*v*)
	Meaning	:	*to mislead money*
	Key	:	DEAF ALL CAT
	Memory link	:	ALL DEAF CAT union complained that people *misled* their *money*.
	Usage	:	Defalcate the funds.
164.	Word	:	**Deleterious** (*adj*)
	Meaning	:	*harmful*
	Key	:	डाल – TREE
	Memory link	:	It is very *harmful* to cut the डाल OF THE TREE on which you are sitting.
	Usage	:	Have a deleterious effect on a child's development.
165.	Word	:	**Derelict** (*adj*)
	Meaning	:	*a person without home*
	Key	:	DAIRY – LICK (चाटना)
	Memory link	:	A person who did not have his home, he was licking at the milk dairy. .
	Usage	:	A derclict living on streets.
166.	Word	:	**Despondency** (*n*)
	Meaning	:	*hopeless; sad*
	Key	:	POND
	Memory link	:	When she became *hopelss*, she went to the POND and sat down in *sad* mood.
	Usage	:	It is very difficult to come out from despondency after his father's death.

167.	Word	:	**Detente** (*n*)
	Meaning	:	*lessening of tension between two countries especially*
	Key	:	THE TENT
	Memory link	:	When *tension between India-Pak* lessened, soldiers started to open THE TENTS on the border area.
	Usage	:	A period of detente.
168.	Word	:	**Detrimental** (*adj*)
	Meaning	:	*harmful*
	Key	:	MENTAL
	Memory link	:	MENTAL People can be *harmful* for you.
	Usage	:	His new activities are detrimental to our policies.
169.	Word	:	**Diabolical** (*adj*)
	Meaning	:	*devilish; very bad*
	Key	:	DIA-DIAMETER, BALL
	Memory link	:	The children were playing with a small BALL. Suddenly the DIAMETER of ball increased to an enormous size and a *devil* came out from it.
	Usage	:	The film was diabolical.
170.	Word	:	**Diffidence** (*n*)
	Meaning	:	*lack of confidence; shyness*
	Key	:	DEN
	Memory link	:	When I asked my friend to enter in the DEN he *lost his confidence.*
	Usage	:	He showed diffidence during the interview.

171.	Word	:	**Dissemble** (*v*)
	Meaning	:	*to pretend; to hide*
	Key	:	DISSEMBLE (OPPOSIT OF ASSEMBLE)
	Memory link	:	In childhood I used to DISSEMBLE lot of things but was unable to assemble again. When my mother would ask me, "Who did this ?" Then I would *pretend or hide* the truth.
	Usage	:	The child dissembling on his mistake.
172.	Word	:	**Dormant** (*adj*)
	Meaning	:	*not active; lazy*
	Key	:	DOOR MAN
	Memory link	:	Our DOOR MAN is very *lazy and not very active person.*
	Usage	:	A dormant volcano.
173.	Word	:	**Draconian** (*adj*)
	Meaning	:	*cruel; servere*
	Key	:	DRACULA
	Memory link	:	A *cruel* DRACULA attacked on the children in the horror movie.
	Usage	:	Draconian laws of Taliban country.
174.	Word	:	**Dolorous** (*adj.*)
	Meaning	:	*sad*
	Key	:	DOLL
	Memory link	:	When his friends snatched his DOLL from the baby, she became very *sad.*
	Usage	:	She was in the dolorous mood.

175.	Word	:	**Decadence** (*n*)
	Meaning	:	*a fall in moral behaviour; art & literature*
	Key	:	DECAY – DECADE
	Memory link	:	Since last DECADE, there was a DECAY in *moral behaviour*, art & literature.
	Usage	:	The decadence of modern society.

TIME : ____________

TEST-7 (151-175)

I. Write down the link words of the following words :

Word	Link
Disport	**This Port (Airport)**
1. Dregs	__________
2. Deride	__________
3. Dotage	__________
4. Distrain	__________
5. Derelict	__________
6. Dyspepsia	__________
7. Draconian	__________
8. Detente	__________
9. Despondency	__________
10. Diaphanous	__________
11. Deranged	__________
12. Dulcet	__________
13. Deleterious	__________
14. Detrimental	__________
15. Diffidence	__________

ANSWER:

1. Drugs, 2. Ride, 3. Dot age, 4. This train, 5. Dairy, lick, 6. Pepsi, 7. Dracula, 8. The tent, 9. Pond, 10. Dial, phone, 11. mountain range, ranger cycle, 12. Dull, set (stage); 13. डाल, Tree, 14. Mental, 15. Den.

II. Tick the synonym of the following words :

1. Dormant
   (a) active (b) inactive
   (c) record (d) learning

2. Dissemble
   (a) think (b) menace
   (c) disturb (d) pretend

3. Dubious
   (a) doubtful (b) sureness
   (c) criticize (d) regulate

4. Disport
   (a) to care (b) to scold
   (c) to sneer (d) to smile

5. Distrain
   (a) distribute (b) to become angry
   (c) to seize goods (d) to make free

6. Dolorous
   (a) an utensil (b) energetic
   (c) sad (d) wooden

7. Dilettente
   (a) wise (b) not skilful
   (c) move (d) hardworking

8. Dotage
   (a) old time (b) future
   (c) childish (d) languishing

9. Diffidence
   (a) calculative (b) promptness
   (c) assurance (d) lack of confidence

10. Diabolical
   (a) baneful (b) devilish
   (c) healthy (d) relation

ANSWERS:

1. (b), 2. (d), 3. (a), 4. (d), 5. (c), 6. (c), 7. (b), 8. (c), 9. (c), 10. (b)

III. Read the sentences, tick the correct answer of *italicized* word :

1. His past background of life is little *dubious*
   (a) interesting
   (b) doubtful
   (c) common

2. I would *descant* with you before allow him to go
   (a) suggest
   (b) accompany
   (c) discuss

3. The landlord imposed *distrain* on poor man for not paying the rent
   (a) action of seizing goods
   (b) force
   (c) criticism

4. Had a *deleterious* effect on his business
   (a) profitable
   (b) harmful
   (c) advantageous for future specially

5. She was in a mood of *despondency*
   (a) joyous
   (b) excited
   (c) hopeless

6. A period of *detente*
   (a) struggle
   (b) lessening the tension
   (c) growth

7. A *dilletente* artist
   (a) skilled
   (b) unskilled
   (c) humorous & funny

8. He was feeling *dyspeptic* after the meal
   (a) bore & sad
   (b) cold
   (c) suffering from indigestion

9. The child was *dissembling* after his failure
   (a) weeping
   (b) pretending
   (c) laughing

10. A *derelict* lives
    (a) without home
    (b) in a beautiful bungalow
    (c) alone in a simple home

ANSWERS:

1. (b), 2. (c), 3. (a), 4. (b), 5. (c), 6. (b), 7. (b), 8. (c), 9. (b), 10. (a).

IV. Please match the following given below :

1. Draconion	(a) sweet sounding
2. Dormant	(b) cruel
3. Deride	(c) transparent
4. Diaphanous	(d) to mislead
5. Dulcet	(e) inactive
6. Defalcate	(f) childish
7. Dotage	(g) fall or decay
8. Decadence	(h) mad
9. Disport	(i) to ridicule
10. Deranged	(j) to smile

ANSWERS :

1. (b), 2. (e), 3. (i), 4. (c), 5. (a), 6. (d), 7. (f), 8. (g), 9. (j), 10. (h)

V. Fill in the blanks with suitable verbs/phrases.

Dormant, dissemble, detrimental, defalcated, deride, deranged, Dotage

1. We should not ___________ after our mistakes rather we should accept it.
2. To ___________ a handicap person is shameful act.
3. He ___________ the company funds.
4. Cigarette smoking is ___________ to health.
5. Our brain has enormous power but the power is in ___________ stage.

ANSWERS :

1. dissemble, 2. deride, 3. defalcate, 4. detrimental, 5. dormant.

176.	Word	:	**Decimate** (*v*)
	Meaning	:	*to destrory / wipe out or kill a large part of*
	Key	:	DECI – MATE
	Memory link	:	My ROOMMATE *wiped out* the large DECIMAL value of pie.
	Usage	:	Disease has decimated the population of rabits.
177.	Word	:	**Devolve** (*v*)
	Meaning	:	*to pass on to another*
	Key	:	VALVE
	Memory link	:	I tightened the pipe on the big gas cylinder VALVE & *passed the gas to another cylinder.*
	Usage	:	More power is to be devoloved to Regional Govt.
178.	Word	:	**Diatribe** (*n*)
	Meaning	:	*a bitter; criticism in speech writing*
	Key	:	TRIBE
	Memory link	:	TRIBAL socities ususally recieve *bitter criticism.*
	Usage	:	Launch a diatribe against the government.
179.	**Word**	:	**Didactic** *(adj)*
	Meaning	:	*for the purpose of teaching*
	Key	:	DECK (MUSIC SYSTEM)
	Memory link	:	I purchased a musical DECK for *teaching* the students because they wanted to made them hear how to improve english.
	Usage	:	My dad is of too didactic nature.

180.	Word	:	**Exculpate** (*v*)
	Meaning	:	*prove guiltless*
	Key	:	AXE–कल–पेट
	Memory link	:	to find out the truth judge ने कल उसका पेट AXE से काटा and ultimately he was *proved guiltless*.
	Usage	:	The Supreme Court exculpated Sanjay Dutt from TADA Case.
181.	Word	:	**Eccentric** (*adj*)
	Meaning	:	*crazy; odd*
	Key	:	EGGS, CENTER
	Memory link	:	That *crazy* people is eating EGGS while standing in the CENTRE of the road.
	Usage	:	Sometimes Nana Patekar become eccentric in the movies.
182.	Word	:	**Eclectic** (*adj*)
	Meaning	:	*selective*
	Key	:	ELECTRIC
	Memory link	:	My dad has very selective nature. He took one hour in *selecting* the ELECTRIC bulbs for our new house.
	Usage	:	Eclectic taste in music and eating.
183.	Word	:	**Elixir** (*n*)
	Meaning	:	*cure all*
	Key	:	ALEXENDER
	Memory link	:	ALEXENDER the great was known for curing *all* the problems of his people.
	Usage	:	An elixir prescribed by doctor.

184.	Word	:	**Encumber** (*v*)
	Meaning	:	*to become burden*
	Key	:	AN कंबल
	Memory link	:	This कंबल is very heavy. It feels like *a burden* on me.
	Usage	:	Travelling is difficult when you're encumbered with heavy suitcases.
185.	Word	:	**Enigma** (*n*)
	Meaning	:	*puzzling*
	Key	:	NAGMA ACTRESS
	Memory link	:	NAGMA *puzzled* with Prabhu Deva. She was wondering how to dance so quickly.
	Usage	:	I have known for many years, but he remains a complete enigma to me.
186.	Word	:	**Eschew** (*v*)
	Meaning	:	*to avoid; to keep away from something deliberately*
	Key	:	CHEW
	Memory link	:	"Avoid CHEWING tobacco" — advised the doctor to the patient.
	Usage	:	I generally exchew on political discussion.
187.	Word	:	**Eulogy** (*n*)
	Meaning	:	*to praise very much*
	Key	:	ये लो जी
	Memory link	:	I was searching my examination card desperately. My servant searched & gave me the card & said, "ये लो जी". I *praised him very much.*
	Usage	:	He read an eulogy on his dead friend. • Eulogies at her memorial service.

188.	Word	:	**Exigency** (*n*)
	Meaning	:	*a situation calling for immediate attention*
	Key	:	EMERGENCY
	Memory link	:	EMERGENCY requires *immediate attention.*
	Usage	:	I have prepared myself for all exigencies of life.
189.	Word	:	**Extol** (*v*)
	Meaning	:	*to praise highly*
	Key	:	EXTRA – TALL
	Memory link	:	The architecture was *praised highly* for constructing EXTRA TALL building.
	Usage	:	He was extolled as a hero.
190.	Word	:	**Effulgent** (*adj*)
	Meaning	:	*shining brilliantly*
	Key	:	A FULL DETERGENT
	Memory link	:	If you apply a FULL DETERGENT to the Sari, it will *shine brilliantly.*
	Usage	:	The effulgent beauty.
191.	Word	:	**Emollient** (*adj*)
	Meaning	:	*soften or soothing agent*
	Key	:	A MOLE-ANT
	Memory link	:	If you want to get rid of the ANT shaped MOLE apply *soothing agent* on it.
	Usage	:	Emollient tone of the boss.

192.	Word	:	**Enormity** (*n*)
	Meaning	:	*a series crime; of great size*
	Key	:	AN NORM (RULE)
	Memory link	:	Breaking A NORM in the Red Alert Area is *a serious crime.*
	Usage	:	The enormity of a challange/decision. The Enormities of Hitlar Regime.
193.	Word	:	**Espouse** (*v*)
	Meaning	:	*support*
	Key	:	SPOUSE
	Memory link	:	SPOUSE is the *support* to each other.
	Usage	:	Our principal is always ready to espouse the students for the worthy cause.
194.	Word	:	**Extricate** (*v*)
	Meaning	:	*to disentangle; to cut*
	Key	:	TREE, CUT
	Memory link	:	The branches of TREE were CUT from the main stem.
	Usage	:	She extricate herself from an unhappy love affair.
195.	Word	:	**Ebullient** (*adj*)
	Meaning	:	*energetic; enthusiastic*
	Key	:	BULL
	Memory link	:	He was walking very slowly. The moment he saw a crazy BULL, he become *energetic* & run away.
	Usage	:	An ebullient director of a local firm.

196.	Word	:	**Enervate** (*v*)
	Meaning	:	*to lose energy; to make somebody loose strength*
	Key	:	NERVE, WEIGHT
	Memory link	:	"Don't put more weight. My right hand's NERVE is loosing every" said the weightlifter to the coach.
	Usage	:	An enervating argument / illness.
197.	Word	:	**Enjoin** (*v*)
	Meaning	:	*to suggest; to advise*
	Key	:	JOIN
	Memory link	:	He *advised* me not to JOIN to the course.
	Usage	:	We were enjoined not to cheat anybody.
198.	Word	:	**Enunciate** (*v*)
	Meaning	:	*Speak clearly.*
	Key	:	NUN (SISTER IN CHURCH), PRONUNCIATE
	Memory link	:	The NUN PRONUNCIATED each word very clearly.
	Usage	:	She enunciated each word.
199.	Word	:	**Ephemeral** (*adj*)
	Meaning	:	*short lived*
	Key	:	अभी मरल (अभी मरा)
	Memory link	:	"ये अभी मर जाएगें। These are *short lived* insects", said Rahul.
	Usage	:	Ephemeral mosquitoes during the rainy season.

200.	Word	:	**Epitaph** (*n*)
	Meaning	:	*Inscription in the memory of dead person*
	Key	:	A P-SHAPED TAP
	Memory link	:	The surgeon is washing the brain of a dead person under A P-TAP so as to read the *inscription in the memory of dead person*.
	Usage	:	I was reading an epitaph on my friend's gravestone.

TIME : ____________

TEST-8 (176-200)

I. Write down the key word of the following phrases/words.

1. Eccentric ____________
2. Exigency ____________
3. Eclectric ____________
4. Enjoin ____________
5. Devolve ____________
6. Didactic ____________
7. Extol ____________
8. Emollient ____________
9. Ebullient ____________
10. Enervate ____________
11. Effulgent ____________
12. Encumber ____________
13. Enigma ____________
14. Eschew ____________

ANSWERS:

1. Eggs – centre, 2. Emergency, 3. Electric, 4. join, 5. Valve, 6. Deck, 7. Extra, tall, 8. A mole-ant, 9. bull, 10. Nerve, 11. full, detergent, 12. An कंबल, 13. Nagna actress, 14. Chew.

II. Match the following words of Table-1 with Table-2

Table-1	Table-2
1. Enunciate	(a) to kill a parger part
2. Devolve	(b) shining brilliantly
3. Decimate	(c) to avoid
4. Eschew	(d) to pass on
5. Exculpate	(e) to advise
6. Eulogise	(f) to prove guiltless
7. Eccentric	(g) to praise
8. Extricate	(h) speak clearly
9. Enjoin	(i) crazy
10. Effulgent	(j) to cut

ANSWERS:

1. (h), 2. (d), 3. (a), 4. (c), 5. (f), 6. (g), 7. (i), 8. (j), 9. (c), 10. (b)

III. Find out the correct answers of given word out of four choices a, b, c, d.

1. Ebullient
   (a) understand (b) confuse
   (c) charge (d) energetic

2. Extol
   (a) to praise (b) enjoyment
   (c) to beguile (d) to fight

3. Extricate
   (a) to soften (b) to fall
   (c) to make free (d) to annoy

4. Enigma
   (a) change (b) stability
   (c) denial (d) puzzle

5. Devolve
   (a) to pass on (b) to passion
   (c) to insist (d) to seize

6. Electric
   (a) selective (b) careless
   (c) qurrelsome (d) harmful

7. Ephemeral
   (a) haplessness (b) support
   (c) short lived (d) criticism

8. Decimate
   (a) to cause (b) to kill
   (c) to calculate (d) to distribute

9. Didactic
   (a) understanding (b) speaking
   (c) teaching (d) harmful

10. Epitaph
    (a) excited (b) An inscription
    (c) romantic (d) emergency

ANSWERS:

1. (d), 2. (a), 3. (c), 4. (d), 5. (a), 6. (a), 7. (c), 8. (b), 9. (c), 10. (b)

IV. Fill in the blanks with suitable word/phrases :

Words: decimate, extolled, enervated, diatribe, devolve, ebullient, didactic, dolorous.

1. We were __________ not to go outside in the winter.
2. After lifting this heavy box I was feeling __________
3. After winning the world cup, Australian team was in __________ mood.
4. He __________ his duties to his assistant because he was on the leave that day.
5. After loosing the competition, she was looking in __________ state.
6. Viswanathan Anand was __________ by the prime minister of India.
7. We need to __________ the increasing population of insects as they are harmful to the crops.

ANSWERS :

1. Enjoined, 2. Enervated, 3. Ebullient, 4. Devolved, 5. Dolorous, 6. Extolled, 7. Decimate.

201.	Word	:	**Equitable** (*adj*)
	Meaning	:	*fair; reasonable*
	Key	:	EQU–EQUAL, TABLE
	Memory link	:	Everybody will get EQUAL place on the TABLE. This is a *fair decision*.
	Usage	:	This was an equitable distribution of wealth.
202.	Word	:	**Excision** (*n*)
	Meaning	:	*the action of cutting/removing something*
	Key	:	OXYGEN
	Memory link	:	The villain *cut* the OXYGEN pipe from the mouth of the actor's mother.
	Usage	:	An excision of report was necessary to bring it down to an acceptable length.
203.	Word	:	**Extirpate** (*v*)
	Meaning	:	*to remove which is undesirable*
	Key	:	Extra पेट
	Memory link	:	*Remove* your EXTRA पेट. It is not desirable. Go for morning walk.
	Usage	:	The practice of dowry must be extirpated.
204.	Word	:	**Extraneous** (*adj*)
	Meaning	:	*coming from outside; unrelated*
	Key	:	EXTRA, US
	Memory link	:	He is an EXTRA player. So he should not be included with us. Also he has *unrelated* skill & nagative attitude.
	Usage	:	My boss cut down all extraneous information from the speech.

205.	Word	:	**Engender** (*v*)
	Meaning	:	*produce; cause*
	Key	:	GENDER (MALE FEMALE)
	Memory link	:	Only GENDERS with opposite sex can *produce* child.
	Usage	:	Poverty engenders crime.
206.	Word	:	**Earthy** (*adj*)
	Meaning	:	*unrefined; coarse*
	Key	:	EARTH
	Memory link	:	The sand particals of this EARTH are *unrefined & coarsed.*
	Usage	:	The very earthy character.
207.	Word	:	**Embellish** (*v*)
	Meaning	:	*to decorate*
	Key	:	BELLY (सैंडिल)
	Memory link	:	My girl friend was *decorating* her BELLY for beating me.
	Usage	:	A dress embellished with lace and ribbons.
208.	Word	:	**Ennui** (*n*)
	Meaning	:	*a feeling of boredom*
	Key	:	A NEW
	Memory link	:	I am *feeling bore* from this cassette. I need a NEW cassette.
	Usage	:	Feeling of ennui in his mind.

209.	Word	:	**Flippant** (*adj*)
	Meaning	:	*flips (leafs or pages of a diary planner); ant*
	Key	:	QUICK CHANGING ATTITUDE
	Memory link	:	A huge ANT was *quickly changing* the FLIPS of a drawing chart.
	Usage	:	A flippant remark / opinion.
210.	Word	:	**Fulminate** (*v*)
	Meaning	:	*protest strongly & loudly*
	Key	:	फल (FRUITS)
	Memory link	:	The housewives were *protesting strongly & loudly* against the vegetable sellers जो सडे फल बेच रहे थे।
	Usage	:	All newspapers fulminated against governments's incompetence.
211.	Word	:	**Febrile** (*adj*)
	Meaning	:	*nervous and little excited*
	Key	:	FEBRUARY MONTH
	Memory link	:	February month is the examination month. Students usually become *nervous & little excited.*
	Usage	:	Febrile pre-election activity.
212.	Word	:	**Fealty** (*n*)
	Meaning	:	*loyalty*
	Key	:	FEEL
	Memory link	:	*Loyalty* can be FELT only.
	Usage	:	The CBI officer took an oath of fealty.

213.	Word	:	**Felicity** (*n*)
	Meaning	:	*great happiness; the quality of well designea, well planned*
	Key	:	फैली (WIDESPREAD)
	Memory link	:	दो CITY बहुत फैली है So I am feeling great *happiness.*
	Usage	:	She illustrated her point with great felicity.
214.	Word	:	**Fatuous** (*adj*)
	Meaning	:	*stupid & silly; foolish*
	Key	:	FAT
	Memory link	:	That FAT *stupid* person was eating in a *silly manner.*
	Usage	:	A fatuous look / remark.
215.	Word	:	**Firebrand** (*n*)
	Meaning	:	*trouble maker*
	Key	:	FIRE
	Memory link	:	He ignited the FIRE in the house. He is a *trouble maker for the colony.*
	Usage	:	A young right-wing firebrand in the college.
216.	Word	:	**Facile** (*adj*)
	Meaning	:	*effortless; not hard to do*
	Key	:	FACE, OIL
	Memory link	:	The drop of OIL was rolling down *effortlessly* from his FACE.
	Usage	:	A facile work / speech.

217.	Word	:	**Fortitude** (*n*)
	Meaning	:	*courage; boldness to face difficulties*
	Key	:	FORT
	Memory link	:	It was an act of boldness to unfurl the flag on FORT before Independence.
	Usage	:	He tolerated the pain with great fortitude.
218.	Word	:	**Fulsome** (*adj*)
	Meaning	:	*(esp of speech or writing) in excessive or of great degree*
	Key	:	FULL – SOME
	Memory link	:	The water glass is already FULL. If you put more it will become *excessive.*
	Usage	:	Fulsome words / compliments.
219.	Word	:	**Fallacy** (*n*)
	Meaning	:	*a false belief; a false argument*
	Key	:	FALSE
	Memory link	:	It was a FALSE *argument.*
	Usage	:	A statement based on fallacy.
220.	Word	:	**Fatalism** (*adj*)
	Meaning	:	*the belief that all events are determined by God & fate*
	Key	:	FATE
	Memory link	:	He used to believe too much on FATE. She would always think that everything is *determined by God & fate.*
	Usage	:	I accepted both good & bad times with fatalism.

221.	Word	:	**Fecund** (*adj*)
	Meaning	:	*productive; fertile*
	Key	:	FEE
	Memory link	:	"The course is very *productive* so dont worry abou the FEE." the counsellor said to the student.
	Usage	:	A fecund imagination.
222.	Word	:	**Figurine** (*n*)
	Meaning	:	*a small ornamental statue*
	Key	:	FIGURE (OF A GIRL)
	Memory link	:	The FIGURE of this girl is looking like *a small ornamental statue.*
	Usage	:	A figurine of Lord Buddha.
223.	Word	:	**Faux pass** (*n*)
	Meaning	:	*a social mistake*
	Key	:	FOX PASS
	Memory link	:	In the marriage of FOX, the invitation PASSES were given to every animal but forgot to invite Lion. It was a big *social mistake!*
	Usage	:	A faux pass in the marriage party.
224.	Word	:	**Functionary** (*n*)
	Meaning	:	*a person with official duties; officer*
	Key	:	FUNCTION
	Memory link	:	In the sports FUNCTION, every officer was alloted a *duty.*
	Usage	:	A minor functionary.

225.	Word	:	**Fiasco** (*n*)
	Meaning	:	*a complete feuture*
	Key	:	FEE ASK
	Memory link	:	When English tutor ASKED for the FEE, students denied because they said they were COMPLETELY FAILED in all the exams.
	Usage	:	My every plan ended in fiasco.

TIME : ____________

TEST-9 (201-225)

I. Write down the key words of the following words. For example the key for "Ebullient" is bull :

1. Engender ____________
2. Extraneous ____________
3. Fiasco ____________
4. Fealty ____________
5. Fecund ____________
6. Fortitude ____________
7. Fulsome ____________
8. Febrile ____________
9. Flippant ____________
10. Firebrand ____________
11. Facile ____________
12. Excision ____________
13. Equitable ____________
14. Felicity ____________
15. Fatuous ____________

ANSWERS:

1. Gender, 2. Extra, us, 3. Fee Ask, 4. Feel, 5. Fee, 6. Fort, 7. Full, some, 8. February month, 9. Flips, 10. Fire, 11. Face, oil, 12. Oxygen, 13. Equal, table, 14. फैली City, 15. Fat.

II. Matching :

1. Functionary	(a) reasonable
2. Equitable	(b) to cause
3. Extirpate	(c) feverish a nervous
4. Engender	(d) A social mistake
5. Febrile	(e) to remove
6. Flippant	(f) excessive
7. Fatuous	(g) officer
8. Fecund	(h) stupid
9. Fulsome	(i) changeable
10. Faux pass	(j) productive

ANSWERS:

1. (g), 2. (a), 3. (e), 4. (b), 5. (c), 6. (i), 7. (h), 8. (j), 9. (f), 10. (d)

III. Multiple Choice :

In each group select the word that is a synonym of the *italicized* word

1. Poverty *engenders* crime
   (a) causes (b) supports
   (c) produce (d) both a & c.

2. An *excision* of extra expenditure
   (a) removal (b) addition
   (c) discussion (d) creation

3. A *figurnine* means
   (a) hide (b) a small statue
   (c) pronounce (d) speak clearly

4. Feeling of *ennui*
   (a) excitement (b) boredom
   (c) courage (d) future planning

5. A very *earthy* character
   (a) unrefined (b) refined
   (c) smart (d) immature

6. A document based on *fallacy*
   (a) crime (b) false argument
   (c) misbehaviour (d) fault

7. *Facile* speech
   (a) lovely (b) excited
   (c) encouraging (d) effortless

8. A man of great *fortitude*
   (a) courage (b) money
   (c) character (d) dignity

9. believe in *fatalism*
   (a) fate (b) eating too much
   (c) spending too much (d) creativity

10. *Fecund* idea

(a) false (b) true

(c) productive (d) none of these

ANSWERS:

1. (a), 2. (a), 3. (b), 4. (b), 5. (a), 6. (b), 7. (d), 8. (a), 9. (a), 10. (c)

226.	Word	:	**Gerrymander** (*v*)
	Meaning	:	*to change voting district lines in order to favour a political party*
	Key	:	गैर (OUTSIDER) – MAN
	Memory link	:	Some BJP supporters were residing in a village which was beyond the district line. *To favour* BJP party during elections, the *administration changed voting district lines.*
	Usage	:	gerrymandering the district lines.
227.	Word	:	**Garrulous** (*adj*)
	Meaning	:	*talking much especially about unimportant things*
	Key	:	गौरिल्ला
	Memory link	:	When he *talks too much especially about unimportant* & silly things, he looks like a गौरिल्ला।
	Usage	:	He became garrulous after a few glasses of wine.
228.	Word	:	**Germane** (*adj*)
	Meaning	:	*relevant*
	Key	:	GERMAN LANGUAGE
	Memory link	:	Our GERMAN language instructor speaks German in a *relevant* way.
	Usage	:	The manager gave remarks that were germane to the discussion.
229.	Word	:	**Glean** (*v*)
	Meaning	:	*to collect (fact etc)*
	Key	:	LEAN (TO BEND)
	Memory link	:	The sugar fell down on the floor. My mom LEANED down & *collected* all the crystals.
	Usage	:	The editor gleaned information from all leading newspapers.

230.	Word	:	**Glut** (*adj*)
	Meaning	:	*over abundance; too much*
	Key		गलत
	Memory link	:	The answer is *too much* गलत।
	Usage	:	The market glutted with cheap apples.
231.	Word	:	**Gourmand** (*n*)
	Meaning	:	*a person who like to eat too much*
	Key	:	GOVERNMENT
	Memory link	:	The greedy officials of GOVERNMENT like to *eat and drink too much.*
	Usage	:	My friend Rajiv is a gourmand.
232.	Word	:	**Grueling** (*adj*)
	Meaning	:	*difficult, tiring & involving great effort*
	Key	:	GRILL
	Memory link	:	The workers are cutting the iron GRILL with a great *difficulty*. It really needs a great effort to cut thick iron rods.
	Usage	:	It was a grueling day for me.
233.	Word	:	**Gambit** (*n*)
	Meaning	:	*a risky action*
	Key	:	GAME
	Memory link	:	In every GAME, one requires to take *risky action.*
	Usage	:	His opening gambit at the debate was excellent.

234.	Word	:	**Genuflect** (*v*)
	Meaning	:	*to bend the knees in worship; to touch the feet*
	Key	:	जानू (FIANCEE) REFLECT
	Memory link	:	My जानू reflected on her knees to *touch the feet* of my parents.
	Usage	:	The priest genuflected before the God.
235.	Word	:	**Gadfly** (*n*)
	Meaning	:	*a person who disturbs others*
	Key	:	FLY
	Memory link	:	Like a FLY you *disturbs* me too much.
	Usage	:	A gadfly was there in our party. It was very difficult to get rid of him.
236.	Word	:	**Gossamer** (*n*)
	Meaning	:	*a very thin, filmi cloth*
	Key	:	DOSSA
	Memory link	:	*Masala* DOSA is looking like a *very thin filmy cloth.*
	Usage	:	She was wearing a gown of gossamer silk.
237.	Word	:	**Graduated** (*adj*)
	Meaning	:	*step by step; move in steps*
	Key	:	GRADUATION (B.A./B.COM)
	Memory link	:	It you want to do GRADUATION, you will have to complete it through *step by step process.*
	Usage	:	He got success in graduated manner.

238.	Word	: **Gullible** (*n*)
	Meaning	: *easily deceived*
	Key	: गरीब
	Memory link	: Rich people आसानी से गरीब लोगों को deceive कर लेते हैं।
	Usage	: Young girls are very gullible in teen age.
239.	Word	: **Gyrate** (*v*)
	Meaning	: *to move in a circular way*
	Key	: जा RATE
	Memory link	: He ordered his servant, "जा RATE पूछ कर आ।" The servant *moved* shop to shop in Connaught Place *in a circular way.*
	Usage	: Dancers gyrating around the floor.
240.	Word	: **Gregarious** (*adj*)
	Meaning	: *fond of company of others / outsiders*
	Key	: GREEK – गैर
	Memory link	: It is known fact that GREEK people गैरों की *company* ज्याद पसंद करते हैं।
	Usage	: She is very outgoing and gregarious.
241.	Word	: **Harangue** (*v*)
	Meaning	: *to criticize loudly & angrily*
	Key	: हरा रंग
	Memory link	: जब मेरी wife हरे रंग की साड़ी पहन कर आई, I *criticized her angrily* because I hate green colour.
	Usage	: My father harangued me due to my failure in examination.

242.	Word	:	**Halcyon** (*adj*)
	Meaning	:	*happy*
	Key	:	HELLO – कौन
	Memory link	:	The mother picked up the phone & said, "Hello कौन" The moment she came to know the phone was of her son from USA, she become *very happy*.
	Usage	:	The halcyon days of one's youth.
243.	Word	:	**Hiatus** (*n*)
	Meaning	:	*a gap*
	Key	:	HATE
	Memory link	:	*A gap* between high status family is widening. I HATE this.
	Usage	:	There will be a two weeks hiatus before the talks can be resumed.
244.	Word	:	**Hirsute** (*adj*)
	Meaning	:	*hairy*
	Key	:	HER-SUIT
	Memory link	:	She is a *hairy* girl. Her long & shining *hairs* are coming down HER SUIT.
	Usage	:	A hirsute dog moving on the road.
245.	Word	:	**Histrionic** (*adj*)
	Meaning	:	*insincere and in humorous way*
	Key	:	History
	Memory link	:	My son was studying HISTORY book in an *insincere & humorous way.*
	Usage	:	History look like a theatrical subject.

246.	Word	:	**Homily** (*n*)
	Meaning	:	*long sermon / religious talk*
	Key	:	HOMELY
	Memory link	:	A HOMELY mother generally passes long *religious talk* to her girl.
	Usage	:	Deliver homilies to their children.
247.	Word	:	**Horrendous** (*adj*)
	Meaning	:	*horrible*
	Key	:	HORN
	Memory link	:	The sound of this HORN is very *horrible*.
	Usage	:	Horrendous problem in our families.
248.	Word	:	**Hortatory** (*adj*)
	Meaning	:	*advising*
	Key	:	HEART
	Memory link	:	After the HEART transplantation, the doctor *advised* him not to move fast.
	Usage	:	Hortatory talks to the employees.
249.	Word	:	**Highfaultin** (*adj*)
	Meaning	:	*foolishly trying to appear too grand*
	Key	:	HIGH FALL
	Memory link	:	My friend was *foolishly trying to appear too grand*. He was planing to FALL from a HIGH building to *show* off the people.
	Usage	:	She gave highfaultin ideas for celeberating Diwali.

250.	Word	:	**Horology** (*n*)
	Meaning	:	*the scicnce of measuring time or making pieces*
	Key	:	HOROSCOPE
	Memory link	:	HOROSCAPE is based on the *science of measuring time*.
	Usage	:	"Have you ever studied Horology?" asked the teacher.

TIME : ____________

TEST - 10 (226-250)

I. Write down the key word for the given words mentioned below :

e.g. Gadfly	**fly**
1. Gambit	__________
2. Gourmand	__________
3. Glean	__________
4. Garrulous	__________
5. Homily	__________
6. Histrionic	__________
7. Hiatus	__________
8. Halcyon	__________
9. Gyrate	__________
10. Genuflect	__________
11. Horrendous	__________
12. Hortatory	__________
13. Functionary	__________
14. Germane	__________

ANSWER :

1. Game, 2. Government, 3. Lean, 4. गौरिल्ला, 5. Homely girl, 6. History, 7. Hate, 8. Hello कौन, 9. जा Rate, 10. Reflect, 11. Horn, 12. Heart, 13. Function, 14. German

II. From the group after each word, select the word or words closest in meaning to the listed :

1. Histrionic
   (a) insincere (b) history
   (c) sincere (d) discouraging

2. Hirsute
   (a) laughable (b) hairy
   (c) command (d) theory

3. Harangue
   (a) colour (b) speech
   (c) sound (d) new word

4. Halcyon
   (a) happy (b) animal
   (c) unstable (d) length

5. Gregarious
   (a) like company of others (b) logical
   (c) willing (d) to lower

6. Gullible
   (a) ancient (b) move slowly
   (c) condition (d) easily decieved

7. Highfaultin
   (a) social mistake (b) boasting & showy
   (c) proud (d) growth

8. Horology
   (a) a novel
   (b) true
   (c) catchword
   (d) a science of measuring time

9. Garrulous
   (a) talkative (b) belief
   (c) unitidy (d) response

10. Glean
   (a) deviate (b) destroy
   (c) to collect (d) make story

ANSWER :

1. (a), 2. (b), 3. (b), 4. (a), 5. (a), 6. (d), 7. (d), 8. (d), 9. (a), 10. (c)

III. Matching :

1. Hiatus	(a) speak angrily
2. Harangue	(b) a person who annoys others
3. Genuflect	(c) a gap
4. Gadfly	(d) in steps

5. Graduated	(e) to bend the knees
6. Gyrate	(f) difficult & tiring
7. Homily	(g) move in circular motion
8. Glut	(h) religious talks
9. Gruelling	(i) too much
10. Gambit	(j) risky action

ANSWER :

1. (c), 2. (a), 3. (a), 4. (b), 5. (d), 6. (g), 7. (h), 8. (i), 9. (f), 10. (j)

IV. Mark 'True' or 'False' for the given sentences :

1. It is good to pass on homilies to our children.(True/False)
2. We cannot glean information from the newspapers. (True/False)
3. A gullible person can be easily deceived. (True/False)
4. He does not like the company of others therefore we call him a gregarious person. (True/False)
5. Hirsuit dogs have soft hair generally. (True/False)
6. A gourmand lives to eat. (True/False)
7. When we remember halcyon days of our. Youth, we feel happy (True/False)
8. True success can be achieved in a graduated manner. (True/False)
9. We should genuflect in front of God (True/False)
10. A hortatory means advice (True/False)

ANSWERS :

1. True, 2. False, 3. True, 4. False, 5. True, 6. True, 7. True, 8. True, 9. True, 10. True.

251.	Word	:	**Idyllic** (*adj*)
	Meaning	:	*peaceful; beautiful*
	Key	:	इडली
	Memory link	:	I saw my friend eating इडली in a *peaceful and beautiful hotel.*
	Usage	:	An idyllic cottage/ scenery.
252.	Word	:	**Imminent** (*adj*)
	Meaning	:	*likely to happen anything wrong*
	Key	:	EMINENT
	Memory link	:	One of the EMINENT astrologer forcasted that *something wrong, likely* to happen in near future.
	Usage	:	Seeing the cloud my friend said. "Rain is imminent."
253.	Word	:	**Impeccable** (*adj*)
	Meaning	:	*faultless; without any mistake*
	Key	:	PACK-CABLE
	Memory link	:	"This electrical wire should be PACKED *faultessly*" ordered the engineer to the worker.
	Usage	:	His written english is impeccable.
254.	Word	:	**Impinge** (*v*)
	Meaning	:	*to collide*
	Key	:	PIN
	Memory link	:	My scooter tyre *collided* with heavy iron PINS.
	Usage	:	It is difficult to prevent problems impinging on your work.

255.	Word	:	**Inclement** (*adj*)
	Meaning	:	*severe*
	Key	:	IMPLEMENT
	Memory link	:	If India wants to control corruption, *severe* IMPLEMENTATION of rules is inevitable.
	Usage	:	Inclement rules for the athletic games.
256.	Word	:	**Idiosyncrasy** (*n*)
	Meaning	:	*a person's particular way of thinking & behaving which is different from others*
	Key	:	IDIOT, CRAZY
	Memory link	:	This person is really an IDIOT & CRAZY. He *behaves & completely different from others.*
	Usage	:	I don't like his idiosyncrasy of criticizing him.
257.	Word	:	**Imbroglio** (*n*)
	Meaning	:	*a complicated situation/ problem*
	Key	:	IN BRA
	Memory link	:	An ant entered IN THE BRA. It became a COMPLICATED SITUATION for her.
	Usage	:	He unnecessarily involved in a boardroom imbroglio.
258.	Word	:	**Impolitic** (*adj*)
	Meaning	:	*not wise*
	Key	:	POLITICS
	Memory link	:	To enter in POLITICS is *not a wise* decision for you.
	Usage	:	It might be impolitic to refuse his order.

259.	Word	:	**Impugn** (*v*)
	Meaning	:	*challenged as false*
	Key	:	नग्न
	Memory link	:	Pooja Bhatt *challanged* the media that her नग्न scenes were false.
	Usage	:	Impugn Somebody's motives.
260.	Word	:	**Incipient** (*adj*)
	Meaning	:	*early time*
	Key	:	IN C.P. (CANNAUGHT PLACE)
	Memory link	:	In early times, I had a small shop in CANNAUGHT PLACE.
	Usage	:	There was a sign of incipient unrest on her face.
261.	Word	:	**Incursion** (*n*)
	Meaning	:	*Lord Curson*
	Key	:	temporary invasion (अत्याचार)
	Memory link	:	LORD CURZON in 18th century had *temporary invasion* on Indians.
	Usage	:	Sudden incursion on the Hindus in Pakistan.
262.	Word	:	**Indefatigable** (*adj*)
	Meaning	:	*tireless*
	Key	:	FATIGUE
	Memory link	:	If you do not feel FATIGUE, you will remain *tireless*.
	Usage	:	An indefatigable compaigner for civil rights.

263.	Word	:	**Indemnity** (*adj*)
	Meaning	:	*make sure against loss*
	Key	:	IN DAM
	Memory link	:	While roaming on the dam, my friend's camera fell down IN THE DAM. I assured him that I shall give another *one against this loss.*
	Usage	:	An indemnity fund to the victims
264.	Word	:	**Inebrity** (*n*)
	Meaning	:	*intoxiacation*
	Key	:	IN ऐब (बुराई)
	Memory link	:	He has only one ऐब – which is *intoxication.*
	Usage	:	Lost in an state of inebrity.
265.	Word	:	**Innocuous** (*adj*)
	Meaning	:	*harmless*
	Key	:	KNOCK, US
	Memory link	:	The boxer applied a severe KNOCK to US on my head but it was *harmless.*
	Usage	:	An innocuous remark.
266.	Word	:	**Insouciant** (*adj*)
	Meaning	:	*without worry*
	Key	:	IN SAUCE-ANT
	Memory link	:	There was an ANT IN the maggi. SAUSE. Without *tension & worry* I ate it.
	Usage	:	Her cheerful insouciant mood

267.	Word	:	**Invective** (*adj*)
	Meaning	:	*abusive language*
	Key	:	IN WAKE
	Memory link	:	My sister was sleeping soundly I cried in her right ear. She WAKED up & started shouting in *abusive language.*
	Usage	:	Let out a stream of invective.
268.	Word	:	**Incontinent** (*adj*)
	Meaning	:	*unable to control the bowels*
	Key	:	CONTINENTAL (FOOD)
	Memory link	:	My brother-in-law ate too much CONTINENTAL FOOD yesterday. Now he is *unable to control the bowels.* The whole day he was in toilet.
	Usage	:	People often become incontinent when they get very old.
269.	Word	:	**Insipid** (*adj*)
	Meaning	:	*tasteless; dull*
	Key	:	SIP
	Memory link	:	I took a SIP of fruit bear. It was quite *tasteless.*
	Usage	:	An insipid performance.
270.	Word	:	**Insurmontable** (*adj*)
	Meaning	:	*untolerable*
	Key	:	SIR, MOUNT
	Memory link	:	Our physical SIR MOUNTED a big, heavy wooden log on my head. It was really *untolerable.*
	Usage	:	The problems are insurmontable.

271.	Word	:	**Irate** (*v*)
	Meaning	:	*very angry*
	Key	:	RATE
	Memory link	:	My uncle became *very angry* when the salesman charged unreasonable RATE of a cold drink.
	Usage	:	Irated customers demanding their money back.
272.	Word	:	**Juxtapose** (*v*)
	Meaning	:	*to place people and things very close to each other*
	Key	:	JUST OPPOSITE
	Memory link	:	My house is *very close* to the temple, - JUST OPPOSITE to the temple.
	Usage	:	juxtapose light and shade in the painting.
273.	Word	:	**Jaunty** (*adj*)
	Meaning	:	*feeling self-confidence*
	Key	:	JAUNTY RODES (SOUTH AFRICAN CRICKETER)
	Memory link	:	I saw JAUNTY RODES in South Africa vs India Cricket Match. What a *confidence* he exhibits during fielding!
	Usage	:	A jaunty tune/ rythm.
274.	Word	:	**Jocund** (*adj*)
	Meaning	:	*pleasant; cheerful*
	Key	:	JOKE
	Memory link	:	My uncle played a JOKE in a *pleasant manner*. Every body was having cheerful smile on the face.
	Usage	:	The little girls jocund manner of speaking were attractive.

275.	Word	:	**Jettison** (*v*)
	Meaning	:	*to throw unnecessary things from a ship aircraft etc.*
	Key	:	JET – SON
	Memory link	:	There were unnecessary things lying on the JET. The captain asked his SON to *throw all unnecessary things* down the jet.
	Usage	:	The tankers were jettisioning crude oil.

TIME : ____________

TEST - 11 (251-275)

I. Write down the key for the given word :

1. Incontinent ____________
2. Irate ____________
3. Jettison ____________
4. Idyllic ____________
5. Impinge ____________
6. Idiosyncrasy ____________
7. Imbroglio ____________
8. Incipient ____________
9. Indemnity ____________
10. Innocuous ____________
11. Invective ____________
12. Inebrity ____________
13. Impolitic ____________
14. Impeccable ____________
15. Impugn ____________

ANSWERS :

1. Continental food, 2. Rate, 3. Jet, son, 4. इडली, 5. Pin, 6. Idiot, crazy, 7. In bra, 8. C.P. (Cannaught Place) 9. In dem, 10. Knock, 11. Wake, 12. In (ऐब), 13. In Politics, 14. Pack cable, 15. Nude (नग्न)

II. Matching :

1. Impeccable	(a) tireless
2. Imbroglio	(b) faultless
3. Impugn	(c) abusive
4. Indefatigable	(d) intoxication
5. Invective	(e) taking challenge as false
6. Inebrity	(f) peaceful & beautiful
7. Idyllic	(g) cheerful & pleasing
8. Inclement	(h) a complicated situation
9. Jocund	(i) a feeling of confidence
10. Jaunty	(j) severe

ANSWERS :

1. (b), 2. (h), 3. (e), 4. (a), 5. (c), 6. (d), 7. (f), 8. (j), 9. (g), 10. (i)

III. Tick the right choice out of four choices :

1. Jocund
   (a) cheerful (b) unacceptable
   (c) creative (d) arrogant

2. Imminent
   (a) likely to (b) happened in
   (c) horrible happen (d) advising past

3. Ignominous
   (a) decorative (b) foolish person
   (c) ungraceful (d) historical

4. Insurmountable
   (a) untolerable (b) homely girl
   (c) character (d) theatrical

5. Indefatigable
   (a) measurement (b) a kind of machine
   (c) altercation (d) tireless

6. Inebrity
   (a) intoxication (b) variety
   (c) nervous (d) excitement

7. Insouciant
   (a) interfere (b) widespread
   (c) trouble (d) carefree

8. Incipient
   (a) a political (b) in eary stage
   (c) an official (d) loyalty person

9. Imbroglio
   (a) quite (b) widespread
   (c) complicated situation (d) open area

10. Idyllic
    (a) sorrow (b) happy
    (c) changing (d) constant

ANSWERS :

1. (b), 2. (a), 3. (c), 4. (a), 5. (d), 6. (a), 7. (d), 8. (b), 9. (c), 10. (b)

276.	Word	:	**Jeremiad** (*n*)
	Meaning	:	*a tale or incident of woe*
	Key	:	जावेद मियाँदाद (PAKISTANI CRICKET PLAYER)
	Memory link	:	JAVED MIANDAD was banned from playing cricket in future. It was really an *incident of woe* for him.
	Usage	:	Her jeremiad about her past suffering made me weep.
277.	Word	:	**Jeer** (*v*)
	Meaning	:	*to laugh rudely*
	Key	:	जीरा
	Memory link	:	Govt. sanctioned Rs 5 lakh for Development of Delhi. This was like "ऊँट के मुँह में जीरा" My sister remarked and *laughed in a rude manner.*
	Usage	:	Jeer at the speaker.
278.	Word	:	**Jersey** (*n*)
	Meaning	:	*a light brown cow which produces high quality milk*
	Key	:	जर्सी
	Memory link	:	*A light brown cow* which produces high quality milk was wearing a जर्सी because it was very cold.
	Usage	:	In USA, you will find lot of Jerseys.
279.	Word	:	**Jib** (*v*)
	Meaning	:	*to refuse; to be unwilling to accept*
	Key	:	जीभ
	Memory link	:	Doctor asked my brother to show his (जीभ) tongue but he *refused plainly*.
	Usage	:	He jibbed when I told him the price.

280.	Word	:	**Jape** (*n*)
	Meaning	:	*a joke played on somebody*
	Key	:	APE (A KIND OF MONKEY)
	Memory link	:	An APE played *a joke on* lioness on her beauty.
	Usage	:	Atal Ji japed on Jailalita in the parliament.
281.	Word	:	**Japonica** (*n*)
	Meaning	:	*an ornamental bush with red flowers and green fruits*
	Key	:	JAPAN
	Memory link	:	"This *decorative ornamental bush* of red flower is from JAPAN. My sister sent it to us yesterday." my aunty said in a boasting manner.
	Usage	:	rare japonica in the lush gardens of South Africa.
282.	Word	:	**Jalopy** (*n*)
	Meaning	:	*an old used car*
	Key	:	जलेबी
	Memory link	:	My brother-in-law was selling जलेबी in his *old car*.
	Usage	:	A jalopy Mercedez Benz.
283.	Word	:	**Jangle** (*v*)
	Meaning	:	*to irritate somebody*
	Key	:	जंगल
	Memory link	:	When I could not get the way of coming out from जंगल. I became irritated.
	Usage	:	Her voice jangled on his ears. Her slow pace jangled her nerves.

284.	Word	:	**Jagged** (*adj*)
	Meaning	:	*with rough pointed often sharp edges*
	Key	:	JUG
	Memory link	:	This JUG has the rough, *sharp edge*. Please lift it carefully.
	Usage	:	Jagged rocks/cliffs.
285.	Word	:	**Jodhpurs** (*n*)
	Meaning	:	*trousers that are loose above the knee and tight from the knee to the ankle worn when riding a horse*
	Key	:	जोधपुर (A DISTRICT OF UTTAR PARDESH)
	Memory link	:	The people of JODHPUR (जोधपुर) district of Uttar Pardesh *wear a special type of trouser* during riding a horse.
	Usage	:	A pair of Jodhpurs.
286.	Word	:	**Juror** (*n*)
	Meaning	:	*a member of a Jury*
	Key	:	जरूर
	Memory link	:	"यह काम आपको जरूर करना है" a member of jury ordered.
	Usage	:	Select the jurors.
287.	Word	:	**Kleptomania** (*n*)
	Mening	:	*an abnormal desire to steal*
	Key	:	CLAP – MAN
	Memory link	:	Whenever this mad MAN hear the CLAPPING sound in a party or anywhere an *abnormal desire to steal* the mobile/stereos etc. triggers in mind.
	Usage	:	A person suffering from kleptomania.

288.	Word	:	**Killjoy** (*n*)
	Meaning	:	*person who destroys other people's enjoyment*
	Key	:	KILL JOY
	Memory link	:	We were enjoying the party but our lecturer KILLED all the JOY. He is really a killjoy.
	Usage	:	He behaves like a killjoy.
289.	Word	:	**Knacker** (*v*)
	Mening	:	*to make somebody very tired*
	Key	:	निक्कर (SHORT PANT)
	Memory link	:	This tight निक्कर made my legs *very tired* because I could not walk comfortably.
	Usage	:	This writing work knackered the whole day.
290.	Word	:	**Lassitude** (*n*)
	Mening	:	*laziness; Lack of energy*
	Key	:	लस्सी
	Memory link	:	After drinking लस्सी, I started feeling lazyiness.
	Usage	:	I felt a sudden lassitude descended on me.
291.	Word	:	**List** (*v*)
	Mening	:	*lean over*
	Key	:	LIST
	Memory link	:	Students were *leaning over* the LIST issued by admission cell of the college.
	Usage	:	Bus was listing badly.

292.	Word	:	**Lampoon** (*v*)
	Meaning	:	*to criticize somebody publicly*
	Key	:	LAMP
	Memory link	:	Sonia Gandhi standing in big LAMP shaped cabin & *criticizing* BJP party in public.
	Usage	:	Her cartoons mercilessly lampooned the leading polititians of the day.
293.	Word	:	**Latitude** (*n*)
	Meaning	:	*freedom to behave or take decisions without restriction*
	Key	:	LATE ATTITUDE
	Memory link	:	"You always come LATE in the office. This is an ATTITUDINAL problem with you. You are not *allowed to take your own decision*", the boss rebuked at the officer.
	Usage	:	They allow their children for too much latitude. I think this is not good for their future.
294.	Word	:	**Leeway** (*n*)
	Meaning	:	*amount of freedom to move or change*
	Key	:	BRUCE LEE-WAY
	Memory link	:	Nobody can come in the WAY of bruce LEE so he has total *freedom to move*.
	Usage	:	Most people have considerable leeway in how they spend their money.
295.	Word	:	**Limbo** (*n*)
	Meaning	:	*in an unfinished & uncertain state*
	Key	:	लम्बा
	Memory link	:	It's already 5 yrs still this लम्बा tower is in *unfinished and an uncertain state.*
	Usage	:	The project was in limbo untill the

			committee made its decision.
296.	Word	:	**Loopy** (*adj*)
	Meaning	:	*crazy*
	Key	:	LOOP
	Memory link	:	My friend made a LOOP of rope, put it around his neck & attempted to suicide. What a *crazy* person he is!
	Usage	:	It sounds a loopy idea to me.
297.	Word	:	**Labyrinth** (*n*)
	Meaning	:	*confusion; maze*
	Key	:	LADY RIN
	Memory link	:	A LADY went to buy a RIN soap & got confused in the market because the market was like a *maze*.
	Usage	:	A person suffering from labyrinth.
298.	Word	:	**Laconic** (*adj*)
	Meaning	:	*brief*
	Key	:	LACK
	Memory link	:	I had LACK of knowledge in politics. So I could give only a brief answer to the employer.
	Usage	:	Laconic humour/answer.
299.	Word	:	**Lapidary** (*adj*)
	Meaning	:	*worker in precious stone factory*
	Key	:	LAP DIARY
	Memory link	:	A *worker in diamond factory* shining the stones in his LAP mentioning in the DIARY the no. of diamonds he worked today.
	Usage	:	The lapidary changed the appearance

			of diamond.
300.	Word	:	**Ludicrous** (*adj*)
	Meaning	:	*laughable*
	Key	:	LOUD – CRY
	Memory link	:	It was *laughable* to see Lalloo Yadav CRYING very LOUDLY during election campaign.
	Usage	:	Ludicrous, ídea.

TEST - 12 (276-300)

I. Write down the key word of the following words for example :

Incontinent	**Continental (food)**
1. Lampoon	________
2. Knacker	________
3. Labyrinth	________
4. Jangle	________
5. Japanoica	________
6. Jalopy	________
7. Latitude	________
8. Jeremiad	________
9. Jeer	________
10. Jagged	________
11. Limbo	________
12. Laconic	________
13. Ludicrous	________
14. Lapidary	________
15. Leeway	________

ANSWERS :

1. Lamp, 2. निक्कर Short Pant, 3. लस्सी, (Lady rin) 4. जंगल, 5. Japan, 6. जलेबी, 7. Late, Attitude, 8. Pakistani Cricket Player, जावेद मियाँदाद, 9. जीरा, 10. Jug, 11. लम्बा, 12. Lack, 13. Loud, cry 14. Lap, diary, 15. Bruce Lee-way.

II. Find out the correct answer out of four choices :

1. Lassitude
   (a) adroit (b) lazy
   (c) active (d) pensive

2. Lampoon
   (a) stupid (b) to quality
   (c) ennui (d) to criticize

3. Jangle
   (a) to irritate (b) to go fast

(c) to stop (d) to amuse

4. Labyrinth
   (a) side by side (b) a machine
   (c) confusion (d) slow collision

5. Lapidary
   (a) conflict (b) wise
   (c) a worker (d) cricketer

6. Jape
   (a) forest (b) a joke
   (c) to hesitate (d) a fruit

7. Jalopy
   (a) old car (b) a sweet dish
   (c) urgent (d) unimportant

8. Loopy
   (a) scheme (b) calm
   (c) free (d) crazy & stupid

9. Latitude
   (a) freedom (b) around the world
   (c) tasteless (d) particular

10. Kleptomania
    (a) desire to jump (b) desire to steal
    (c) planning to move (d) desire to eat

ANSWERS :

1. (b), 2. (d), 3. (a), 4. (c), 5. (c), 6. (b), 7. (a), 8. (d), 9. (a), 10. (b)

III. Match the following words of Table-1 with Table-2

Table - 1	Table - 2
1. Japonica	(a) A member of Jury
2. Jeremiad	(b) to lean over
3. Juror	(c) Sharp edges
4. Jagged	(d) A person who annoys others
5. Killjoy	(e) Laughable

6. Labyrinth (f) confusion, maze
7. Ludicrous (g) A story of woe
8. Leeway (h) freedom to change
9. Limbo (i) An ornamental bush
10. List (j) unfinished

ANSWERS :

1. (i), 2. (g), 3. (a), 4. (c), 5. (d), 6. (f), 7. (e), 8. (h), 9. (j), 10. (b)

IV. Read the sentences & find out whether the sentence is 'True' or 'False'.

1. A kleptomaniac has abnormal desire to steal. (True/False)
2. We cannot eat insipid food happily (True/False)
3. When we lampoon a person, we criticize him in public. (True/False)
4. If something jangles you, you feel relaxed & comfortable. (True/False)
5. When a student jibs at making speech he is willing preparing & accepting it. (True/False)
6. The disappointed fans of cricket started jeering at the players when they loose the match. (True/False)
7. A ludicrous solution means very sincere & appropriate solution. (True/False)
8. Jodhpurs is a special kind of shirt. (True/False)
9. When a ship lists it means it is leaning on one side. (True/False
10. Painting were juxtaposed with other photographs mean they were put separately (True/False)

ANSWERS :

1. True, 2. True, 3. True, 4. False, 5. False, 6. True, 7. False, 8. False, 9. True, 10. False

II. Fill in the blanks with suitable word/phrase :

Words : Labyrinth, Limbo, Ludicurous, Lassitude, Laconic, Loopy, Latitude, Lampoon

1. Parents should not allow their children for too much ____________________.

2. I felt a sudden ________________ descended on me.
3. In movie Sholay, Amitabh Bachhan used to give ________________ answers.
4. The construction is in ________________ due to lack of finance.
5. My crazy friend gave a ________________ idea of earning money.
6. "Laloo Yadav will become prime minister". It is a ________________ talk.
7. Union leader speech ________________ the strict & unlawful owners of the company
8. In those congested area, of old Delhi we lost in the ________________ of the streets.

ANSWERS:

1. Latitude, 2. Lassitude, 3. Laconic, 4. Limbo, 5. Loopy, 6. Ludicuros, 7. Lampooned, 8. Labyrinth.

TIME : ______ ____

301.	Word	:	**Macabre** (*adj*)
	Meaning	:	*horrible*
	Key	:	मकबरा
	Memory link	:	It seems very *horrible* to visit any मकबरा in the night.
	Usage	:	What a macabre incident!
302.	Word	:	**Moribund** (*adj*)
	Meaning	:	*death; come to an end completely*
	Key	:	मोरी (passage), बंद (close)
	Memory link	:	Suddenly all the मोरी (passage) of taking breath became बंद (closed). So he *died* immediately.
	Usage	:	A moribund civilization/economy.
303.	Word	:	**Motility** (*n*)
	Meaning	:	*movement*
	Key	:	मोटी लड़की
	Memory link	:	It is very difficult for that मोटी लड़की even to *move*.
	Usage	:	Quit India was a great motility.
304.	Word	:	**Machination** (*n*)
	Meaning	:	*a secret and complicated plan*
	Key	:	MACHINE
	Memory link	:	Dawood Ibrahim purchased MACHINE guns for & some explosion under a *secret & complicated plan*.

	Usage	:	Political machinations.
305.	Word	:	**Malinger** (*v*)
	Meaning	:	*to pretend to be ill in order to avoid work*
	Key	:	माली (GARDNER)
	Memory link	:	Our माली (gardener) is *pretending to be ill* because he does not want to work today.
	Usage	:	The officer malingering his duty.
306.	Word	:	**Manger** (*n*)
	Meaning	:	*a long open box from which horses & cattle can feed*
	Key	:	MANAGER
	Memory link	:	My *manager* was eating the straw in *a long open box.*
	Usage	:	The baby Jesus lay in a manger.
307.	Word	:	**Mercenary** (*n*)
	Meaning	:	*selfish; mainly concerned with making money*
	Key	:	MERCY
	Memory link	:	The *selfishman* showed no MERCY on the poor man.
	Usage	:	Society accused of mercenary.
308.	Word	:	**Mercurial** (*adj*)
	Meaning	:	*inconstant; quick to change*
	Key	:	MERCURY
	Memory link	:	"The MERCURY has *quick-to-change* characteristic", the chemistry teacher told the students.

	Usage	:	With mercurial attitude, nobody can get succeess.
309.	Word	:	**Mete** (*v*)
	Meaning	:	*distribute*
	Key	:	MEET (ATHLETIC MEET)
	Memory link	:	In the athletic MEET our principal *distributed* the prizes to the winners.
	Usage	:	Principal meted out the certificates to the student.
310.	Word	:	**Meticulous** (*adj*)
	Meaning	:	*careful*
	Key	:	MAT
	Memory link	:	My servant was cleaning the MAT of drawing room very *carefully*.
	Usage	:	Meticulous research in the laboratory.
311.	Word	:	**Militate** (*v*)
	Meaning	:	*work against*
	Key	:	MILITANT
	Memory link	:	The MILITANTS always work against the country.
	Usage	:	Pakistani soldiers militate against India.
312.	Word	:	**Misgiving** (*n*)
	Meaning	:	*worried, anxiety about the consequences, result*
	Key	:	MISS (A GIRL), GIVING
	Memory link	:	Though she (MISS) was giving a kiss to me but she was looking more *worried* about the consequences of it.

	Usage	:	I have serious misgivings about my job.
313.	Word	:	**Misnomer** (*n*)
	Meaning	:	*wrong use of name or word or description*
	Key	:	NAME – MISSED
	Memory link	:	The TV anchor MISSED my NAME in program firstly and later she *wrongly* pronounced.
	Usage	:	'Luxury hotel' was a complete misnomer for the dilapidated building we stay in.
314.	Word	:	**Mountebank** (*n*)
	Meaning	:	*pretender (बहाने मारने वाला)*
	Key	:	BANK ON MOUNT EVEREST
	Memory link	:	He is real a pretender. Yesterday he was saying that he had his BANK account on MOUNT Everest.
	Usage	:	You should not believe on him. He is a mountebank.
315.	Word	:	**Mundane** (*adj*)
	Meaning	:	*uninteresting; dull*
	Key	:	MONDAY
	Memory link	:	Sunday is interesting but MONDAY is always *uninteresting & dull.*
	Usage	:	I do not like his mundane style of speaking or writing.
316.	Word	:	**Munificient** (*adj*)
	Meaning	:	*generous, large in amount*
	Key	:	मुनि
	Memory link	:	Apparently, all the मुनि looks *generous*

			& kind to us.
	Usage	:	A munificent gift/ banefactor.
317.	Word	:	**Myopia** (*n*)
	Meaning	:	*inability to plan for future*
	Key	:	MY-O-पिया
	Memory link	:	Lover is saying to his girl friend "O MY पिया, please don't leave me becuase of my *inability to plan for future*."
	Usage	:	The prevalent educational myopia at national level.
318.	Word	:	**Mortified** (*v*)
	Meaning	:	*to humiliate*
	Key	:	मोटी FIGHT
	Memory link	:	This मोटी girl is in a habit of FIGHTING everyday and this brings lots of humiliation to her family.
	Usage	:	He felt mortified on an issue against him.
319.	Word	:	**Machievellian** (*adj*)
	Meaning	:	*clever deceitful tricks*
	Key	:	MATCH – VILLAIN
	Memory link	:	Only the VILLAINS of a cricket MATCH are using *clever and deceitful tricks.*
	Usage	:	Machivellian policies nowadays.
320.	Word	:	**Martinet** (*adj*)
	Meaning	:	*strict disciplinarian*
	Key	:	मारती (Beat)
	Memory link	:	This school principal Madam बच्चों को बहुत मारती है। She is really strict

321.	Word	:	**Maudlin** (*adj*)
	Meaning	:	*foolishly crying & sentimental*
	Key	:	MODELLING
	Memory link	:	Many young girls join MODELLING. But when they don't get success they *foolishly cry & became sentimental.*
	Usage	:	The maudlin emotions in the movie failed to inspire the audiences.
322.	Word	:	**Minutiae** (*n*)
	Meaning	:	*small details*
	Key	:	MINUTE
	Memory link	:	My boss wants every *small detail* of every MINUTE of my work.
	Usage	:	Leave the minutiaes for future discussion.
323.	Word	:	**Moratorium** (*n*)
	Meaning	:	*legal suspension or delay; a temporary stay*
	Key	:	मोड़ा-तोड़ा (Twist)
	Memory link	:	In India, legal cases को मोड़-तोड़ कर *delay* कर दिया जाता है।
	Usage	:	Declare a moratorium on commercial agreement.
324.	Word	:	**Nebulous** (*adj*)
	Meaning	:	*not clear; cloudy*
	Key	:	नींबू रस (LEMON JUICE)
	Memory link	:	This नींबू रस is *not clear*. Give me another.
	Usage	:	The manager presented a nebulous plan.

325.	Word	:	**Nettle** (*v*)
	Meaning	:	*to make somebody slightly angry; to irritate*
	Key	:	NET
	Memory link	:	When I trapped him in the NET, he became *slighty angry & irritated.*
	Usage	:	My remarks clearly nettled her.

TIME : ___________

TEST - 13 (301-325)

I. Write down the keys of the following words. For example :

'Motility'	**मोटी (a fat woman)**
1. Munificient	__________
2. Meticulous	__________
3. Manger	__________
4. Moratorium	__________
5. Misgiving	__________
6. Mete	__________
7. Militate	__________
8. Myopia	__________
9. Mortified	__________
10. Machievellian	__________
11. Misnomer	__________
12. Martinet	__________
13. Moribund	__________
14. Malinger	__________
15. Macabre	__________

ANSWERS :

1. मुनि saints, 2. Mat, 3. Manager, 4. मोरा तोड़ा, 5. Mis giving, 6. Athletic Meet, 7. Militants, 8. My-O-पिया, 9. मोट्टी Fight, 10. Match Villain, 11. Miss name, 12. मारती (Beat), 13. मोरी (Passage), (close) 14. gardener, 15. मकबरा।

III. Match the following :

1. Mercenary	(a) annoyed
2. Nettle	(b) working against
3. Nebulous	(c) legal delay
4. Militate	(d) anxiety about result
5. Moratorium	(e) pretender
6. Misgiving	(f) selfish
7. Loopy	(g) tearfully sentimental
8. Maudlin	(h) not clear
9. Mountebank	(i) strict disciplinarian
10. Martinet	(j) crazy

ANSWERS :

1. (f), 2. (a), 3. (h), 4. (b), 5. (c), 6. (d), 7. (j), 8. (g), 9. (e), 10. (i)

IV. Tick the correct meaning of the following *italicized* words.

1. *Mundane views*
   (a) Imaginative (b) Creative
   (c) Critical (d) Uninteresting

2. *Mercenary*
   (a) desire for fight (b) Interested in making money
   (c) Commanding (d) Love for helping others

3. *Machination of politics*
   (a) Secret schemes (b) Special Machines
   (c) Principles (d) Redressing system

4. *Mortified*
   (a) Satisfactory (b) Understandable
   (c) defending (d) humilated

5. *Munificient*
   (a) A saint (b) designed floor
   (c) timely (d) cautious

6. *Minutiae*
   (a) attitude (b) loyalty
   (c) unimportant matter (d) supply in excess

7. *Meticulous research*
   (a) careful (b) not concerned
   (c) imaginative (d) clairvoyance

8. *Mountebank person is one who*
   (a) pretends (b) criticizes
   (c) disguises (d) encourages others

9. *Macabre*
   (a) movement (b) a medicine
   (c) horrible (d) an idler

10. *Mercurial*
    (a) constant (b) quick to move
    (c) slow (d) a liquid

ANSWERS :

1. (d), 2. (b), 3. (a), 4. (d), 5. (c), 6. (c), 7. (a), 8. (a), 9. (c), 10. (b)

326.	Word	:	**Nexus** (*n*)
	Meaning	:	*connection*
	Key	:	NECK
	Memory link	:	The boxer broke the *connection* of NECK from the head of the refree.
	Usage	:	There is an evil nexus between police & gangsters.
327.	Word	:	**Necromancy** (*n*)
	Meaning	:	*black magic; magic of communicating with dead bodies*
	Key	:	CROW – MAN
	Memory link	:	Through his *black magic*, the magician converted a *man* into *crow*.
	Usage	:	Practising necromancy.
328.	Word	:	**Noisome** (*adj*)
	Meaning	:	*unpleasant*
	Key	:	Noise
	Memory link	:	*Unpleasant* NOISE in the factory, made me annoyed.
	Usage	:	noisome smell in the bathroom.
329.	Word	:	**Nostrum** (*n*)
	Meaning	:	*questioning on a medicine; something questionable*
	Key	:	NOSE – DRUM
	Memory link	:	After taking antibiotic medicine for cough my NOSE swelled to the shape of a DRUM. Then I *questioned* myself whether it was *a right medicine or not.*
	Usage	:	A nostrum prescribed by a doctor.

330.	Word	:	**Nefarious** (*adj*)
	Meaning	:	*very wicked*
	Key	:	फेरी (वाला)
	Memory link	:	This फेरीवाला who was selling balloons to children is *very wicked.*
	Usage	:	Nefarious policies /activities.
331.	Word	:	**Nonchalance** (*n*)
	Meaning	:	*not showing anxiety; appearing calm & relaxed*
	Key	:	NO चालान (A LEGAL PUNISHMENT)
	Memory link	:	Traffic Policeman ने चालान कर दिया। But my friend was calm & relaxed. There was *no anxiety* on his face.
	Usage	:	He received the trophy with nonchalance.
332.	Word	:	**Nepotism** (*n*)
	Meaning	:	*favouritism; the practicing of favouring their reletives*
	Key	:	NAP (A SHORT SLEEP)
	Memory link	:	Politician's relatives can have A NAP in the office but no other employee was allowed. This is called open *favourtism.*
	Usage	:	Achieve promotion through nepotism.
333.	Word	:	**Overt** (*adj*)
	Meaning	:	*open to view, not secret*
	Key	:	OVER
	Memory link	:	The meeting is OVER. Now it is *open to view.*
	Usage	:	An overt display of jealousy.

334.	Word	:	**Opulence** (*n*)
	Meaning	:	*wealth*
	Key	:	OPEL (ASTRA) LANCER CAR
	Memory link	:	My neighbour bought OPEL Astra & LANCER cars. He has too much *wealth.*
	Usage	:	Living a life in opulence.
335.	Word	:	**Ostensible** (*adj*)
	Meaning	:	*on surface; clear*
	Key	:	TENSION
	Memory link	:	TENSION was clear on the child's *surface.*
	Usage	:	There was an ostensible anxiety on his face.
336.	Word	:	**Ostracize** (*v*)
	Meaning	:	*to exclude from; to remove*
	Key	:	EXTRA SIZE
	Memory link	:	The salesman *removed* all the EXTRA SIZE shirts.
	Usage	:	He was ostracized from the meeting for his rude behaviour.
337.	Word	:	**Odyssey** (*n*)
	Meaning	:	*a long adventurous journey*
	Key	:	VIP ODYSSEY BRIEFCASE
	Memory link	:	I bought a VIP ODYSSEY BRIEFCASE for a *long adventurous journey.*
	Usage	:	Moving for an odyssey.

338.	Word	:	**Opportune** (*adj*)
	Meaning	:	*timely*
	Key	:	OPPORTUNITY
	Memory link	:	OPPORTUNITIES come. But you need to cash them on *right time*.
	Usage	:	Arrive at opportune moment.
339.	Word	:	**Ostentatious** (*adj*)
	Meaning	:	*showy*
	Key	:	उस TENT
	Memory link	:	उस TENT को देखो कितना *showy* है।
	Usage	:	Ostentatious decoration in the marriage party.
340.	Word	:	**Oniomania** (*n*)
	Meaning	:	*intense desire to buy the things*
	Key	:	ONION
	Memory link	:	My aunty *has intense desire* to buy ONIONS of various kind from round the world.
	Usage	:	Suffering from oniomania.
341.	Word	:	**Obfuscate** (*v*)
	Meaning	:	*to confuse*
	Key	:	अब फंस गए
	Memory link	:	"अब फंस गए, समझ नहीं आ रहा" — I am *confused*.
	Usage	:	He accused the government of obfuscating the issue

342.	Word	:	**Occident** (*n*)
	Meaning	:	*west*
	Key	:	ACCIDENT
	Memory link	:	A brutal ACCIDENT in the WEST Delhi - 200 people died.
	Usage	:	News from the occident.
343.	Word	:	**Ordain** (*v*)
	Meaning	:	*to order; to command*
	Key	:	और दे
	Memory link	:	The officer *ordered* the salesman, "और दें मुझे — Give me more."
	Usage	:	Fate had ordained that they would never meet again.
344.	Word	:	**Pandemonium** (*n*)
	Meaning	:	*chaos; disorder*
	Key	:	पंडे, मुनि
	Memory link	:	सारे पंडे और मुनियों ने *chaos* मचा रखा है।
	Usage	:	There was a lot of pandemonium in the class.
345.	Word	:	**Parsimonious** (*adj*)
	Meaning	:	*stingy; money minded*
	Key	:	PURSE
	Memory link	:	He is a *money minded* person. He will not put out his PURSE from his pocket.
	Usage	:	Parsimonious fellow.

346.	Word	:	**Perfidious** (*adj*)
	Meaning	:	*false; deceitful*
	Key	:	बर्फी
	Memory link	:	He was very *deciteful* & *false*. उसने मुझे जूठे मुझे से बर्फी खिला दी।
	Usage	:	Perfidious influence on the society of the politicians nowadays.
347.	Word	:	**Petrify** (*v*)
	Meaning	:	*to make somebody frightened completely*
	Key	:	PAT ON BACK (पीठ पर थपथपाना)
	Memory link	:	Yesterday night when my father PATTED ON MY BACK, I was *completely frightened.*
	Usage	:	Seeing a Cobra, he was petrified.
348.	Word	:	**Polemic** (*n*)
	Meaning	:	*full of controversy*
	Key	:	POLE
	Memory link	:	In Olympics, 'POLE throw' competition was *full of controversies.*
	Usage	:	Unnecessary engaged in polemic issue.
349.	Word	:	**Preposterous** (*adj*)
	Meaning	:	*absurd; ridiculous*
	Key	:	POSTER
	Memory link	:	This obscene POSTER is quite absurd and *ridiculous.*
	Usage	:	His suggestions was quite preposterous.

			preposterous.
350.	Word	:	**Puerile** (*adj*)
	Meaning	:	*childish*
	Key	:	PURE
	Memory link	:	A *child* is always PURE.
	Usage	:	He was behaving in a puerile manner.

TEST - 14 (326-350)

I. Please write down the key word of the following words

'Nebulous' **नींबू रस (lemon juice) :**

1. Occident ____________
2. Ordain ____________
3. Parsimonius ____________
4. Pandemonium ____________
5. Perfidious ____________
6. Nexus ____________
7. Nostrum ____________
8. Nonchalance ____________
9. Obfuscate ____________
10. Ostentatious ____________
11. Ostensible ____________
12. Nepotism ____________
13. Petrify ____________
14. Opulence ____________
15. Ostracize ____________

ANSWERS :

1. Accident, 2. और दे, 3. Purse, 4. पंडे और मुनि, 5. बर्फी, 6. Neck, 7. Drum, 8. No, चालान, 9. अब फंस गए, 10. उस Tent, 11. Tension, 12. Nap (a short sleep), 13. Pat on back, 14. Opel Astra, & Lencer Car, 15. Extra size.

II. Match the words with their correct meanings :

1. Petrify	(a) indifference
2. Nexus	(b) connection
3. Nonchalance	(c) west
4. Occident	(d) absurd & dirty
5. Oniomania	(e) controversial
6. Polemic	(f) open to view
7. Preposterous	(g) childish
8. Overt	(h) scared totally

9. Puerile	(i) command
10. Ordain	(j) desire of buying a lot

ANSWERS :

1. (h), 2. (b), 3. (a), 4. (c), 5. (j), 6. (e), 7. (d), 8. (f), 9. (g), 10. (i)

III. Tick the correct answer :

1. *Noisesome* smell means
   (a) pleasant
   (b) unpleasant
   (c) cheerful

2. *Nexus* between police & politians
   (a) connection
   (b) agreement
   (c) amendment

3. She gave *preposterous* idea during the meeting
   (a) convincing
   (b) absurd & awkward
   (c) wonderful

4. *Nefarious* man means
   (a) very wicked
   (b) very wealthy
   (c) honest

5. She practices *necromancy*
   (a) black magic
   (b) fashion designing from old items
   (c) being silent

6. *Perfidious* statement
   (a) false
   (b) special comment
   (c) argumentative remarks

7. A *nostrum* is a
   (a) unpleasant situation
   (b) false evidence
   (c) ineffective medicine

ANSWERS :

1. (b), 2. (a), 3. (b), 4. (a), 5. (a), 6. (a), 7. (c)

IV. Write down the meanings of the words/ phrases for example :

Word	Meaning
Nonchalance	*Calm & Relaxed*
Nefarious	*Wicked*
1. Puerile	________
2. Occident	________
3. Odyssey	________
4. Overt	________
5. Nepotism	________
6. Nostrum	________
7. Noisome	________
8. Opportune	________
9. Ostracize	________
10. Obfuscated	________

ANSWERS :

1. Childish. 2. West, 3. A journey, 4. Open to view, 5. Favouritism, 6. Questionable medicine, 7. Unpleasant, 8. Timely, 9. To remove, 10. Confused.

			TIME : ___________
351.	**Word**	:	**Ratify** (*v*)
	Meaning	:	*verify*
	Key	:	RAT
	Memory link	:	My mom was *verifying* the place where the RAT died.
	Usage	:	The police ratifying the situation.
352.	Word	:	**Ravenous** (*adj*)
	Meaning	:	*extremely hungry*
	Key	:	रावण (RAVAN)
	Memory link	:	RAVAN was *extremely hungry* for Sita.
	Usage	:	A ravenous appetite.
353.	Word	:	**Recalcitrant** (*n*)
	Meaning	:	*stubborn*
	Key	:	CALCI (CALCULATOR)
	Memory link	:	The students were very stubborn. They didn't stop using CALCI (calculator) despite the principal's warning.
	Usage	:	a recalcitrant child.
354.	Word	:	**Redolent** (*adj*)
	Meaning	:	*smelling strongly of something*
	Key	:	RED – LAWN
	Memory link	:	This lawn is *smelling strongly* of RED roses.
	Usage	:	The office was having redolent of

		furniture polish.
355.	Word	: **Refrain** (*v*)
	Meaning	: *resist; to stop oneself doing something*
	Key	: RAIN
	Memory link	: The horse was *resisting* to move in the RAIN.
	Usage	: He refrained himself from cigarettes.
356.	Word	: **Repertoire** (*n*)
	Meaning	: *skills that a person has*
	Key	: (रैपर) OF A TOFFEE OR CHOCOLATE
	Memory link	: This designer has great *skill of* designing any रैपर OF A TOFFEE.
	Usage	: The development of verbal repertoire of young children.
357.	Word	: **Rider** (*n*)
	Meaning	: *change; amendment*
	Key	: RIDER
	Memory link	: *Change* this RIDER he is an unexperienced fellow.
	Usage	: We would like to add a rider to the previous remarks.
358.	Word	: **Rife** (*adj*)
	Meaning	: *full or widespread*
	Key	: RIFLE (GUN)
	Memory link	: RIFLE was *full* with 6 bullets.

	Usage	:	An area where crime is rife.
359.	Word	:	**Ruminate** (*v*)
	Meaning	:	*to think deeply; to meditate*
	Key	:	ROOM, ATE
	Memory link	:	My father was EATING in the *room* & *thinking deeply* about my sisters marriage.
	Usage	:	Ruminating on a serious issue.
360.	Word	:	**Rankle** (*v*)
	Meaning	:	*to irritate; to cause angry feeling*
	Key	:	RANK – UNCLE
	Memory link	:	When I secured low RANK in the class, my UNCLE became so *irritated* on me.
	Usage	:	This incident happened twenty years ago, but it still rankles in my mind.
361.	Word	:	**Rectitude** (*adj*)
	Meaning	:	*morally correct behaviour*
	Key	:	RECK (REGIONAL ENGG. COLLEGE KURUKSHETRA)
	Memory link	:	Mahavir Jain co-author of this book has done engineering from RECK. He has *morally correct behaviour.*
	Usage	:	Atal ji our Prime Minister — a man of examply rectitude.
362.	Word	:	**Reticent** (*adj*)
	Meaning	:	*reserved; not showing his thoughts readily*
	Key	:	RAT – SCENT
	Memory link	:	There RAT SCENT bottle are *reserved* for rats.

	Usage	: The manager was reticent about his plans.
363.	Word	: **Reverie** (*n*)
	Meaning	: *day dream; lost in pleasant thoughts*
	Key	: RIVER
	Memory link	: I was *lost in pleasant thoughts* near the RIVER.
	Usage	: He was in deep reverie when I knocked the door.
364.	Word	: **Risque** (*adj*)
	Meaning	: *(of a story) rude and shocking*
	Key	: RISK
	Memory link	: It was very *shocking* to know that the plane in which we were travelling was having a RISK of crashing.
	Usage	: The biography which raised criticism because of risque paragraph about India.
365.	Word	: **Rabid** (*adj*)
	Meaning	: *violent & extreme (of feeling)*
	Key	: RABBIT
	Memory link	: When RABBIT came to know that tortoise has won the race, he became violent.
	Usage	: Rabid hate against Pakistan.
366.	Word	: **Rapacious** (*adj*)
	Meaning	: *greedy*
	Key	: RAPE

367.	Word	:	**Ratiocination** (*n*)
	Meaning	:	*the process of logical reasoning*
	Key	:	RATIO
	Memory link	:	Find out the RATIO of profit & loss through the *process of logical* reasoning.
	Usage	:	The excellent ratiocination made his argument more believable.
368.	Word	:	**Recondite** (*n*)
	Meaning	:	*difficult to understand*
	Key	:	कौन DIET
	Memory link	:	"पतले होने के लिए कौन-सी लेनी चाहिए" – This is difficult to understand.
	Usage	:	This is the recondite writings of an english author.
369.	Word	:	**Redress** (*v*)
	Meaning	:	*to correct something which is wrong*
	Key	:	DRESS
	Memory link	:	The dress was not stictched properly. I ask him to correct it.
	Usage	:	You should redress your errors.
370.	Word	:	**Remonstrate** (*v*)
	Meaning	:	*protest*
	Key	:	DEMONSTRATE
	Memory link	:	The drivers were *protesting* against CNG fuel so they had DEMONSTRATION in front of Parliament House Yesterday.
	Usage	:	We remonstrated with the neighbours about the noise.

371.	Word	: **Reprehensible** (*adj*)
	Meaning	: *deserving blame*
	Key	: REFREE HENSI CRONJE OF SOUTH AFRICA
	Memory link	: "HENSI CRONJE *deserves blame*," said the match REFREE.
	Usage	: Your attitude is most reprehensible.
372.	Word	: **Restive** (*adj*)
	Meaning	: *difficult to control; uncomfortable*
	Key	: REST
	Memory link	: I was feeling *uncomfortable*. So I took REST for sometime.
	Usage	: Crowd became increasingly restive.
373.	Word	: **Rhapsodize** (*v*)
	Meaning	: *to speak or write in an exaggerated manner*
	Key	: RAP (MUSIC) – DIE
	Memory link	: While listening RAP MUSIC, he kept on writing & SPEAKING in an exaggereted manner. Leter he DIED.
	Usage	: The way he rhapsodized was extremely irritating.
374.	Word	: **Rancor** (*n*)
	Meaning	: *bitter and angry feeling*
	Key	: RAN – कर (TAX)
	Memory link	: It is very *bitter and angry feeling* to know that people try to RUN away from paying their कर (tax).
	Usage	: There was rancor in his voice / eyes.

375.	Word	:	**Recant** (*v*)
	Meaning	:	*to reject*
	Key	:	RE-CAN (PEPSI CAN)
	Memory link	:	When she requested again for the Pepsi Can, I rejected her request.
	Usage	:	Recant his former opinion in public.

TIME : ___________

TEST - 15 (351-375)

I. Find out the key from the given phrases/words for example :

Preposterous — **Poster**

1. Rapacious ______
2. Ratiocination ______
3. Recondite ______
4. Redress ______
5. Remonstrate ______
6. Redolent ______
7. Ratify ______
8. Reverie ______
9. Rabid ______
10. Ravenous ______
11. Rife ______
12. Rankle ______
13. Reticent ______
14. Reprehensible ______
15. Restive ______

ANSWERS :

1. Rape, 2. Ratio, 3. कौन Dite, 4. Dress, 5. Demonstrate, 6. Red (Rose), 7. Rat, 8. River, 9. Rabbit, 10. Raven, 11. Rifle, 12. Rank, 13. Rat, scent, 14. Refree Hensi Crowne 15. Rest.

II. Matching :

1. Ratify	(a) smell
2. Redolent	(b) skill
3. Repertoire	(c) morally correct
4. Rife	(d) day dreaming
5. Rectitude	(e) reserve
6. Reticent	(f) improper
7. Risque	(g) verify
8. Recondite	(h) to reject
9. Rankle	(i) unable to understand
10. Recant	(j) full of
11. Reprehensible	(k) deserving blame
12. Reverie	(l) irritate

ANSWERS:

1. (g), 2. (a), 3. (b), 4. (j), 5. (c), 6. (e), 7. (f), 8. (i), 9. (l), 10. (h), 11. (k), 12. (d).

III. Tick the correct meaning of the following words/phrases :

1. Rider
   (a) change (b) confuse
   (c) applause (d) to plead

2. Rankle
   (a) to enjoy (b) to irritate
   (c) to understand (d) to get a good rank

3. Repertoire
   (a) relation (b) widespread
   (c) Skill that a person has (d) winding person has

4. Rectitude
   (a) correct behaviour (b) pleasant
   (c) reserve nature (d) violent

5. Reverie
   (a) sad mood (b) day dreaming
   (c) affordable (d) opportunity

6. Rabid
   (a) sincere (b) opposite
   (c) violent (d) calm

7. Rife
   (a) recall (b) oppose
   (c) deny (d) full of

8. Rancor
   (a) Irritation (b) crazy
   (c) generous (d) disorder

9. Rhapsodize
   (a) to encourage
   (b) to write or speak in an exaggereted manner
   (c) to explain totally
   (d) to meet deeply separately

10. Redress
    (a) bitter remarks (b) to solve
    (c) to consider (d) to allow

ANSWERS :

1. (a), 2. (b), 3. (c), 4. (a), 5. (b), 6. (c), 7. (d), 8. (a), 9. (b), 10. (b)

IV. Fill in the blanks with the correct words in the given sentences.

Words : Rankled, Ratiocination, Reticent, Recalcitrant, Ratify, Ravenous, Ordained, Rabid, Refrained, Rider, Reverie.

1. I really like the ____________ in his argument.
2. He is a ____________ follower of Islam.
3. She ____________, "outside immediately."
4. ____________ means daydreaming & fantasizing.
5. He is a ____________ child. He doesn't obey me.
6. Bitter experiences of the past ____________ my mind.
7. My wife was ____________ abour her early affair with someone.
8. The horse ____________ to move in the rain.
9. We need to ____________ this case because it has taken a mysterious turn.
10. My ____________ boss has a greed for money.

ANSWERS :

1. Ratiocination, 2. Rabid, 3. Ordained, 4. Reverie, 5. Recalcitrant, 6. Rankled, 7. Reticent, 8. Refrained, 9. Ratity, 10. Ravenous.

V. Write down the meaning of the given words. For example :

Risque	**Improper**
1. Rider	____________
2. Ravenous	____________
3. Rabid	____________
4. Repertoire	____________
5. Rectitude	____________
6. Ruminate	____________
7. Polemic	____________
8. Preposterous	____________
9. Pandemonium	____________
10. Recondit	____________

ANSWERS :

1. Amendment, 2. Extremely hungry, 3. violent, 4. skill, 5. Morally correct behaviour, 6. to think over, 7. Controversial, 8. Absurd, dirty, 9. disorder, 10. difficult to understand.

376.	Word	:	**Refractory** (*adj*)
	Meaning	:	*unmanageable*
	Key	:	FACTORY
	Memory link	:	The fire in the FACTORY became *unmanageable*. Even the fire brigades could not control it.
	Usage	:	A refractory boy. Trying to control his refractory pony.
377.	Word	:	**Relegate** (*v*)
	Meaning	:	*dismiss; to give somebody a lower rank*
	Key	:	रैली – GATE
	Memory link	:	The employees who were involved in रैली on the the main GATE were degraded from their present ranks & *were given lower rank.*
	Usage	:	I have been relegated to the role of a mere assistance.
378.	Word	:	**Repartee** (*n*)
	Meaning	:	*quick & clever commen/reply*
	Key	:	PARTY
	Memory link	:	In the PARTY meeting, Sushma Swaraj gave a *quick & clever* comment on Sonia's criticism.
	Usage	:	Be good at repartee.
379.	Word	:	**Replenish** (*v*)
	Meaning	:	*to fill some thing again*
	Key	:	RE – PLAN
	Memory link	:	The drunkard man was RE-PLANNING to *fill his glass again.*
	Usage	:	Replenish his stock of pet food.

380.	Word	:	**Resurgent** (*adj*)
	Meaning	:	*reviving; getting a new life*
	Key	:	SURGEON
	Memory link	:	SURGEON gave a *new life* to the patient after operation.
	Usage	:	A resurgent economy hope.
381.	Word	:	**Retrench** (*v*)
	Meaning	:	*cut down*
	Key	:	WRENCH
	Memory link	:	With the pipe WRENCH, the plumber cut down the pipe.
	Usage	:	Forced the company to retrench the employees.
382.	Word	:	**Ribald** (*adj*)
	Meaning	:	*rude & humorous remark*
	Key	:	BALD
	Memory link	:	My friend put a *rude & humorous* remark on that BALD man.
	Usage	:	Ribald remarks on the politians.
383.	Word	:	**Rotundity** (*adj*)
	Meaning	:	*roundness*
	Key	:	ROTI
	Memory link	:	ROTI is round.
	Usage	:	Rotundity complextion.

384.	Word	:	**Rubicund** (*adj*)
	Meaning	:	*high coloured (of a person's face or complexion)*
	Key	:	RUBY
	Memory link	:	Ruby Bhatia's face is of high coloured.
	Usage	:	His rubicund face shows that his health is good.
385.	Word	:	**Randy** (*adj*)
	Meaning	:	*sexually excited*
	Key	:	रंडी
	Memory link	:	After seeing a रंडी, my friend became *sexually excited.*
	Usage	:	Feel randy.
386.	Word	:	**Ricochet** *(v)*
	Meaning	:	*to bounce back as a bullet off a wall*
	Key	:	ROCKET
	Memory link	:	The ROCKET *bounced* back after taking off the ground.
	Usage	:	My plans ricocheted badly.
387.	Word	:	**Rookie** (*n*)
	Meaning	:	*an inexperienced person*
	Key	:	रुक
	Memory link	:	इससे गाड़ी बार-बार रुक-रुक रही है – This is an *inexperienced* driver.
	Usage	:	A police rookie.
388.	Word	:	**Salacious** *(adj)*
	Meaning	:	*lustful; having sexual interest*
	Key	:	साले (BROTHER-IN-LAW)
	Memory link	:	मेरे साले are very lustful.
	Usage	:	He was indulged in salacious gossip.

389.	Word	:	**Sinuous** (*adj*)
	Meaning	:	*winding; roundabout*
	Key	:	SIGN (SIGNATURE)
	Memory link	:	My father's SIGNATURE is very *winding*. Hardly anyone can understand what is written.
	Usage	:	Sinuous routes of hilly area.
390.	Word	:	**Sojourn** (*n*)
	Meaning	:	*sleep. Journey*
	Key	:	TEMPORARY STAY
	Memory link	:	In the long *jouney* everbody started to *sleep*. So I decided to take TEMPORARY STAY.
	Usage	:	A brief sojourn in the mountains.
391.	Word	:	**Sedulous** (*adj*)
	Meaning	:	*hardworking; diligent*
	Key	:	SAD
	Memory link	:	Despite lot of *hard work* she lost the game. Then she became very SAD.
	Usage	:	She is doing a sedulous research.

392.	Word	:	**Slander** (*n*)
	Meaning	:	*defamation*
	Key	:	CYLINDER
	Memory link	:	CNG Gas CYLINDER. Issue was a *defamation* for BJP's image.
	Usage	:	Julia bring a slander action against Harry.
393.	Word	:	**Spectral** (*adj*)
	Meaning	:	*ghostly*
	Key	:	TVS SPECTRA BIKE, SPECS
	Memory link	:	Driving SPECTRA bike after wearing black SPECS, my friend looks like a *ghost*.
	Usage	:	This building is known for the spectral beings.
394.	Word	:	**Subjugate** (*v*)
	Meaning	:	to conquer; to win
	Key	:	सब जो GATE
	Memory link	:	"सब जो GATE पर जाएंगे, they will win" said the teacher.
	Usage	:	Alexender wanted to subjugate all nations on the earth.
395.	Word	:	**Supplant** (*v*)
	Meaning	:	*replace*
	Key	:	सब – PLANT
	Memory link	:	My mom *replaced* ALL (सब) PLANTS from indoor to outdoor during rainy season.
	Usage	:	Plants can be grown indoors by supplanting natural light by artificial one.

396.	Word	:	**Tenacious** (*adj*)
	Meaning	:	*stubborn, (जिद्दी)*
	Key	:	TEEN (TEENAGER)
	Memory link	:	In the TEENAGE, teenagers are very *stubborn.*
	Usage	:	The tenacious nature of the officer • tenacious approach for winning the game.
397.	Word	:	**Torpor** (*n*)
	Meaning	:	*habitual idleness* (खाली रहने की आदत)
	Key	:	तोड़-फोड़
	Memory link	:	खाली रहते वक्त तोड़-फोड़ ही सूझती है।
	Usage	:	You will have to wake up from this torpor if you wish to achieve something in your life.
398.	Word	:	**Tyro** (*n*)
	Meaning	:	*beginner*
	Key	:	TYRE.
	Memory link	:	My younger brother does not know how to change the TYRE of the car. He is a *beginner.*
	Usage	:	He is tyro in this export business.
399.	Word	:	**Tremulous** (*adj*)
	Meaning	:	*timid (डरपोक)*
	Key	:	TREE – MULE
	Memory link	:	Seeing a him a *timid* MULE hid himself behind the TREE.
	Usage	:	With a tremulous hand, she accepted the bribe.

400.	Word	:	**Thwart** (*v*)
	Meaning	:	*to oppose a plan /an attempt*
	Key	:	THE WAR
	Memory link	:	In THE WAR, Pakistan was *opposing* our every *attempt* to destroy their buildings.
	Usage	:	Difficulties thwarted my all plans.

TEST - 16 (376 - 400)

I. Write down the key words of the following words :

1. Sinuous ____________
2. Relegate ____________
3. Ribald ____________
4. Ricochet ____________
5. Rookie ____________
6. Sojourn ____________
7. Thwart ____________
8. Subjugate ____________
9. Sedulous ____________
10. Slander ____________
11. Torpor ____________
12. Recant ____________
13. Repartee ____________
14. Resurgent ____________
15. Randy ____________

ANSWERS:

1. Sign (Signature). 2. रैली, gate, 3. Bald, 4. Rocket, 5. रूक, 6. सों, Journey, 7. The War, 8. सब जो gate, 9. Sad. 10. Cylinder, 11. तोड़-फोड़, 12. Can (Pepsi Can), 13. Party, 14. Surgeon, 15. रंडी (A Prostitute).

II. Match the words with their correct meanings

1. Refractory	(a) rude & humorous remark
2. Relegate	(b) to degrade the position
3. Ribald	(c) beginner
4. Spectral	(d) winding
5. Tyro	(e) stubborn
6. Supplant	(f) ghostly
7. Rubicund	(g) reddish
8. Ricochet	(h) sexually excited
9. Thwart	(i) inexperienced person
10. Randy	(j) oppose a plan

11. Rookie (k) replace

12. Sinuous (l) bounce back

ANSWERS:

1. (e), 2. (b), 3. (a), 4. (f), 5. (c), 6. (k), 7. (g), 8. (l), 9. (j), 10. (h), 11. (i), 12. (d)

III. Tick the correct meaning which is closet to the give below words :

1. Relegate
   (a) to disparage (b) to lower the position
   (c) to promote (d) to encourage

2. Replenish
   (a) to fill again (b) to visit
   (c) to scold (d) to mesh

3. Rookie
   (a) a pilot (b) a drunkard
   (c) a skilled person (d) an inexperienced person

4. Sojourn
   (a) critic (b) arrest
   (c) building (d) temporary stay

5. Tenacious
   (a) stubborn (b) hard to believe
   (c) revival (d) dejection

6. Tremulous
   (a) stupid (b) intelligent
   (c) timid (d) bold

7. Spectral
   (a) award (b) specs
   (c) ghostly (d) summer

8. Tyro
   (a) beginner (b) politicians
   (c) experienced (d) coward

9. Rubicund

(a) simple (b) reddish

(c) a place (d) an animal

10. Refractory

(a) humorous (b) controlled

(c) unmanageable (d) roundness

ANSWERS:

1. (b), 2. (a), 3. (d), 4. (d), 5. (a), 6. (c), 7. (c), 8. (a), 9. (b), 10. (c)

IV. Tick the right answer of the italicized words :

1. A *rotundity* figure

(a) round

(b) awkward

(c) small

2. The company is *retrenching* the employees

(a) promoting

(b) cuting down

(c) praising

3. A *resurgent* hope

(a) new

(b) sad

(c) false

4. She was good at *repartee*

(a) decoration

(b) kitchen work

(c) quick & clever reply

5. Slander action

(a) defamation

(b) appropriate

(c) risky

6. *Salacious* interest
   (a) sexual
   (b) casual
   (c) helping to other

7. He is a *tyro* in this business
   (a) inexperienced
   (b) experienced
   (c) pioneer

8. My all plans were *thwarted* by the Govt. new policy
   (a) opposed
   (b) supported
   (c) banefited

9. *Tremulous* approach
   (a) timid
   (b) bold
   (c) wise

10. *Supplant* all the things
   (a) bought
   (b) replaced
   (c) sold

ANSWERS :

1. (a), 2. (b), 3. (a), 4. (c), 5. (a), 6. (a), 7. (a), 8. (a), 9. (a), 10. (b)

SOME TESTIMONIALS FROM THOSE WHO GOT A BREAKTHROUGH IN THEIR LIFE

Mr. Mahavir Jain,

I compliment you for conducting a wonderful program on NLP on 3rd December 2001. These Three hours which, **I have devoted during the peak time of my studies, brought a difference in my life and change in my attitude.**

With millions of thanks to you and NLP. With love....

PREETI, Student, Ryan International School, Faridabad.

Mr. Jain

Before coming here I thought that life was very tough but after this motivational & NLP workshop I am feeling confident. Now I am ready to face the problems. **Life is no more difficult for me.**

AMIT SINGLA, Student DPS, Faridhbad.

I felt delighted to know the working of my brain through Mr. Mahavir Jain. **Now I will try to amend myself by opting various tricks of keeping myself confident through NLP for my bright future.**

HIMANSHU, Student

The 3 hours NLP class held on 3rd Dec. 2001 was really excellent. I never heard such **useful programme ever in life. Every word, every example was inciting a desire to change myself.** This programme will help my life to live in a wonderful way.

SASHI MOONDHARA, Housewife.

The NLP workshop was a rare experience of my life. Till the age of 56. **I never attended such kind of programme.** This lecture stimulated me as not to pass on the blame to others and accept things as they are and try to face them. This is because I have scientifically understood my brain.

V.K. SOMANI, Buisnessman.

The programme on attitude & NLP was excellent. In today's time everybody is highly tensed due to various reasons or others. This NLP workshop will definitely help the people in solving their problems.

After the NLP workshop I have changed a lot and I feel that rest of my life will be very very happy & excited.

M. BAJORIA, Executive.

& many & many more praise

Over 4000 people have attended Mahavir's various programmes on

"Brain & Memory"

Positive Zone (Regd.) Presents
DYNAMIC MEMORY

PRESENTATION AND WORKSHOPS

Dynamic memory presentation and workshop is the outcome of the author's endeavour to optimise the brain capacity to learn faster and retain longer by scrupulous blending of mnemonics and law of control association.

The program is customised for Indian conditions and tailored to suit the critical needs of Government Establishment, Corporates, Clubs, Schools, Colleges, Universities and other Organizations.

Biswa's mission of creating a mentally literate planet— a world where people know how to memorise and remember efficiently, is driven by his passion for honing and mastering the tools of memory. That is why media says: "Biswaroop is a memory genius who has penchant for breaking records." (Indian Express May, 18, 1997.)

Now these invaluable programmes and workshops are available through various Associates spread across the country.

Website : www.dynamicmemory.com
email: biswaroop@yahoo.com
Head office : Positive Zone (Upma: President)
A-23, Sector-11, Faridabad.
Mobile : (Delhi) 9811139474, 9810426909
Branch office : 18E / IB, Padma Pukar Road, Calcutta-92
Phone : 033-4116325
Mumbai : Phone : 022-8176144
Chandigarh : Phone : 0172-601816.
Allahabad : Sachdeva Coaching Centre.
Phone : 0532-460810, 460820

MEMORY MAKER MAGAZINE

A unique monthly guide to better memory, this monthly magazine can help in updating you with the latest development in memory improvement all over the world besides giving you insight in the following areas:

- Speed mathematics techniques
- Developing the emotional quotient
- Effective stress and overcoming worries
- Leading a healthy life naturally
- Confidence building
- Unusual facts
- Developments round the world
- Positive thinking.

Subscribing to the magazine will not only help in enriching your life with the above topics but also will bring you closer to positively motivated people through our MEMORY MAKER CLUB.

SUBSCRIPTION FORM

Please enter my subscription for Memory Maker for the term I have indicated below:

SUBSCRIPTION RATES

Years	No. of Issues	Cover Price	Subscription Rates	Your Saving
One Year	12	Rs. 120	Rs. 100	Rs. 20
Two Year	24	Rs. 240	Rs. 190	Rs. 50

Term : (Please tick): One Year ☐ Two Year ☐
(PLEASE USE CAPITAL LETTERS)

Name : ....
Designation .... Date of Birth. ....
Address..
....
....
Pin Code .... Ph:..
I enclose the Cheque / Demand Draft No. ....
dated .... of Rs. .... favouring *Adventure Multimedia Pvt. Ltd.* payable at New Delhi.

Post to

MEMORY MAKER

406, Dream Land House, 1/18-B,
Asaf Ali Road, New Delhi-02
Phone: 3232562

Please add Rs. 20 — For outside Delhi Cheques.

You May Use a Photo Copy of this Form.

%

www.ingramcontent.com/pod-product-compliance
Lightning Source LLC
LaVergne TN
LVHW041210150826
845673LV00001B/346

* 9 7 8 8 1 7 1 8 2 9 4 4 6 *